# Seduction and spice

*Photography by Herb Schmitz*
*Food styling by Rudolf Sodamin and Pat Doyle*

# Seduction and spice

## 130 recipes for romance

**Rudolf Sodamin**

RIZZOLI
NEW YORK

First published in the United States of America in 1999 by
Rizzoli International Publications, Inc.
300 Park Avenue South,
New York NY 10010

Copyright © 1999 by Rizzoli International Publications, Inc.

Photography copyright © Rudolf Sodamin and Herb Schmitz

LC 99-70707
ISBN 0-8478-2215-X

On front cover: Chocolate Mousse, page 123

Designed by Peter Yates, NYC

Printed in Singapore

*To my sons, Magnus and Kenneth, my wife, Bente, and our new baby girl, Kristina Sophia, the wonderful outcome of "seduction and spice."*

# contents

# Acknowledgments

*f or their support and inspiration I would like to thank: Sirio Maccioni and family; Le Cirque 2000, New York; Jacques Pépin, T.V. master chef; Michael and Ariane Batterberry from* Food Arts *magazine; Andrew Shotts and Tina Tartar; Arkardy Panchernikov from Caviar Russe, New York; Cecilia Schnoor from Maveko Hotel Supply, Hamburg, Germany; Gretel Beer; Karl Winkler; Josef Jungwirth; Mike Smith; Stein Kruse; Gustav Mauler; Bob and Eva Lape, travel writers and gourmets; Ernie and Jim; Angel Antin; Monica Velgos; Melissa Moyal; Julie Mautner; Manfred Ursprunger; Adam Goldstein; Herb Schmitz and Pat Doyle from International Photography, London; Solveig Williams; Marta Hallett; Peter Yates; and Royal Caribbean International.*

# Author's Note

*a* *phrodite, in all her golden, sensual glory, inspired me to write this book. But she was not alone.*

*The idea of an aphrodisiac cookbook has haunted me, flirtatiously darting in and out of my mind, for years. Like a temptress, the concept has teased me, coquettishly calling out to me while I'm selecting fresh fruits and vegetables, pinching the border of a pie crust, or staring into the eyes of my lovely wife, Bente. I leave the moment and pick up a pen, only to find that the fleeting vixen-idea has escaped me yet again. Enchanting, wily thing. Like the love goddess herself, creativity loves a good game of hide-and-seek, for what follows the chase is the greatest satisfaction.*

*Food has brought me such personal and professional joy. A chef bursts with passion for food, not only for the inanimate ingredients—however alive they once were—but with the craving to share artful food with others who appreciate it and to bring them the same bliss. A chef may shyly peek between the kitchen's swinging doors or boldly swagger out in a white ten-button jacket to greet the patrons. One gauges the evening's relative success by the guests' reactions: "Did they feel it? Did I convey the joy?"*

*There is no less delight in cooking for two than in cooking for two hundred or two thousand, as I've done for royalty and heads of state around the world aboard the QE2 or as I presently do aboard Royal Caribbean International. In fact, preparing a romantic meal with Bente as my co-chef delivers as much gratification as cooking for royalty—maybe more. That is because love itself is the ultimate aphrodisiac.*

*Following is my personal collection of aphrodisiac recipes, facts, and lore gleaned from my travels around the globe, chance conversations with other food lovers, and diverse readings. With these words and images, I present food in a new light—food as fantasy, as love catalyst, as art. I hope to inspire you to roll up each other's sleeves, head for the kitchen, and express your feelings through food. And most of all, like any good chef, I want to share with you my joy.*

*—Rudi Sodamin*
*Coral Gables, Florida 1999*

# Introduction

*f*ood and sex are venerated as sacred rites in every world religion. Sustenance and procreation. How could two things so primal, so essential for propagation of the species, also nourish the soul? How could they shape and be shaped by art, culture, and faith? The earliest peoples recognized their magic and sought to unleash their power by controlling the when, the where, and the with whom.

Food evolved as humans became more sophisticated; hunters and gatherers became herders and farmers; food became cuisine. Likewise, sex, the act of procreation, became "making love"—the ultimate expression of one's feelings. And one's effect on the other did not go unnoticed. Foodstuffs provided the energy to make love; they provided a sense of well-being and a yen to embrace a lover— some edibles more than others. Sharing in the preparation and partaking of food brings men and women together like no other act—a concept so intrinsic that Adam and Eve's transgression of the flesh was euphemized by their munching on an apple. The traditions of food and sex have grown as intertwined as wild vines, and as tangled as a sleeping couple's limbs.

Cooking and eating set the stage for romance. You knead pizza dough together; you feel it yield softly beneath your floured fingers. You both feel the rush of heat as you peer in the oven; your heads touch lightly as you insert a fork to test for doneness. You blow on a spoonful of soup at the stove; you hold it out for your lover to sample. "More salt?" Perhaps you uncork a bottle of wine and discuss its merits, comparing its color, bouquet, and texture to vintages you've shared before. One sip brings back the collective memory of an evening long ago and sparks a nostalgic conversation. You set the table, light candles, and toss the salad. These traditions—in addition to your own—create an appealing atmosphere. Somehow the food tastes better on your good china, and you find yourselves relaxed and reconnected.

Can you also experience a romantic evening eating take-out from cardboard containers while watching Monday Night Football? You bet, and don't let anyone tell you differently. Nevertheless, a candlelit dinner at home can be the ultimate inspiration for intimacy, as each ritualistic step arouses anticipation for delights that follow dessert.

For as long as people have sought to enhance sexual pleasure by stirring desire, building stamina, intensifying orgasm, and retaining virility, they have turned to aphrodisiac substances for help. And for as long as couples have yearned for children—the fruits of their passion—they have relied on aphrodisiacs in the form of foods, ointments, potions, and charms. Sensual food is as old as time itself.

Discoveries of many stimulating substances were inadvertent, while other foods were categorized as aphrodisiacs because of their appearance. The ancients believed that food resembling human body parts actually fostered their wellness, especially foods resembling the penis, testes, and vagina—peeled water chestnuts, oysters, bananas. They also held that consuming the meat of virile animals, such as hare, would afford them the same untamed potency. Sometimes a food's reputation was tied to its texture, taste, or aroma. Rare and exotic foods in particular also caused excitement, including ingredients that made their way along established trade routes and those procured from previously unknown lands. Items such as sea spawn, which binds the nests of sea swallows, was used to make Bird's Nest soup, a celebrated Chinese aphrodisiac.

Storytellers wove myths and legends to explain the phenomena of food and passion, blurring science, history, and folklore; the story of Persephone in Greek mythology is one such example. Hades tempted Persephone, the beautiful daughter of Zeus and Demeter, into eating a lusty, forbidden pomegranate seed. He then punished her by forcing her to spend six months of each year in the underworld. Each spring Persephone would return to Earth, marking the return of pomegranates and springtime and linking food and the rebirth of nature together inextricably. Interestingly, a recent study of traditional aphrodisiacs showed that there is some truth behind these myths by demonstrating the general nutritional value of these foods, as well as their profound and positive effect on reproductive health.

From Aphrodite, the name of the Greek goddess of love, beauty, and sexual rapture, stems the English word for lust-inducing material: aphrodisiac. Born of passionate emotion, the fabled goddess is as multifaceted as love itself. Aphrodite is associated with the gay laughter of infatuation, the joy of committed devotion, and the dark side of possessive love. Hesiod, the Greek writer who documented the history of the gods and creation, wrote of her origins in the ninth century B.C. Cronus castrated his father, Uranus, then hurled the severed genitals into the sea, which began to churn violently. From the sea foam—aphros—rose Aphrodite in all her splendor. Of course, the oral tradition furnishes diverse versions of the story. Some say the goddess rose from the sea on an oyster shell, and Homer, the Greek epic poet of the same era, called the goddess the daughter of Zeus and Diane. She was married to Hephaestus the smith, who wrought her a magical girdle of gold filigree in which no god or mortal could resist her charms—perhaps a warning to generous husbands everywhere. The Greeks revered Aphrodite's fertile feminine energy and asked for her support in bearing children and cultivating their crops and gardens. Her lovers were many, and if one should display the least reluctance, Aphrodite also possessed omnipotent insight with respect to stimulating substances—aphrodisiacs.

The ancient Greeks and Romans followed suit and searched for perfect aphrodisiacs to give them sexual vigor in their libertine festivals and orgies. Such substances commanded a high price. Some were ludicrous (wolf penises, deer semen, mythological flowers), while others were highly nutritious foods that are discussed in the sidebars in this book.

The ancient Hindus of India also regarded lovemaking as an intrinsic part of life. Hindi records indicate that Indian men feasted on the native eggplant to boost their sexual stamina as early as the tenth century. Their religious texts and temples also address love-making accordingly. The classic text is the **Kama Sutra** by Vatsayana, compiled from many other works sometime between the third century B.C. and the third century A.D. **Kama**, or sexual fulfillment, refers to one of the three life goals that lead to the ultimate liberation of the soul, along with truth and right conduct (**dharma**) and pursuit of material goods (**artha**). The book also contains recipes to attract others; some are ridiculous, but many are wholesome, if complicated.

On the other hand, the Arabs treated sexuality as an almost academic pursuit. The many preserved writings by learned men (historians, doctors, scholars) are very explicit. The most important is **The Perfumed Garden**, written by the Tunisian Sheik Umar ibn Muhammad al-Nefrawi in the late fourteenth or early fifteenth century. Like the **Kama Sutra**, **The Perfumed Garden** addresses many of the timeless issues lovers face: courting, flirting, kissing, scenting the body, and enlarging and shrinking the sex organs.

Chinese aphrodisiacs, however, have had a mysterious, and often dangerous, reputation throughout history. For example, bamboo shoots, a Chinese aphrodisiac often added to meat dishes, owe their roguish reputation to the fact that some varieties are extremely poisonous—even the edible varieties must be boiled for 10 to 15 minutes to rid them of their toxins. Herbalists who sold potions containing rare and exotic ingredients guarded their secret recipes carefully. This is still reflected in the Chinese aphrodisiacs of today; the demand in China is high for concoctions containing parts of endangered animals and illegal substances such as opium.

The diverse societies of Africa had their share of aphrodisiacs too. Many of those documented took the form of charms and incantations rather than foods. The aphrodisiacs of medieval Europe also took on nontraditional forms and were associated with magic and witchcraft. They gained popularity during the Crusades, which introduced new ideas on sexuality. European potions were notoriously macabre, often containing human excrement, urine, blood, and parts of corpses. The sex organs and fluids of animals were also believed to stimulate the libido. Thankfully, trade with the East and the New World introduced tasty new foods and spices to Europe, and these were later adopted as favorite aphrodisiacs.

It is noteworthy that people living oceans and cultures apart, often with little or no knowledge of each other, esteemed many of the same foods for their aphrodisiac properties. This reflects the development of trade and migration but also points to the likelihood that certain foods do indeed bring about a physical and psychological reaction that invites coition. Over hundreds of years, humans have observed these effects and learned to prepare and combine foods to their advantage. After all, people's aspirations change little over centuries and geography: to find true love, to soar to the summits of sexual pleasure, to multiply, to be free from worry—in a word, to be happy.

*Seafood, vegetables, hot peppers, and chocolate alone do not constitute the key to fabulous sex and happiness; however, the pleasures of the table are an integral part of a healthy lifestyle incorporating exercise, sufficient sleep, humor, and a sense of purpose. The sensory delights of food stimulate the imagination. Dining provides the chance to pause, to linger and daydream, to fantasize over visual, tactile, and fragrant stimuli. A shared meal evokes a sense of mutual gratification that lays the groundwork for fulfillment of a more intimate nature. Our forebears from around the world have discovered that some foods are more provocative than others. With a nod from the scientific and medical communities, beliefs once relegated to the genre of "wives' tales" now carry more weight. And the aphrodisiac recipes once handed down from generation to generation are now prescribed by physicians, nutritionists, and sex therapists—not to mention adventurous chefs.*

*Even cynics who doubt the plausibility of veritable aphrodisiacs admit that the act of breaking bread together is an appetizing form of foreplay. The table is such an obvious meeting point that couples overlook it after the first few dates. Ah, you slurped long strands of spaghetti and dabbed tomato sauce from each other's chins. The waiter suggested Chianti. One of you suggested a movie later. Those were the days, right? Back when you had time. Does it ever seem as though delectable food and earth-moving sex no longer fit into your hectic schedule?*

*Food and sex are so elemental that you might forget to make time for them. These are the days of drive-through windows and cable TV in every bedroom. People are busy and stressed, for technology that promised less work instead created a faster, more demanding world with more to do. News flashes warn of the latest dangers of food; each week another "discovery" is found with another food to ban from your diet. (And the following week researchers discover that that same food will cure a dreaded disease!) And as for sex …well, who has the energy?*

*Grab your calendar and a pen. (No, not a pencil.) Put these on your to-do list now: Cook. Dine together. Look into each other's eyes. Remember why you fell in love in the first place. Hold hands. Make love. Soon.*

*The intent of* **Seduction and Spice** *is to serve as a springboard. It is not encyclopedic; instead it offers some of my favorite, most sensual recipes, adapted for your home kitchen. Meditating on the photos, text, and directions will get your own creative juices flowing and put you in the mood to stir up something wonderful tonight. Ponder this innuendo-laden proverb of the lusty French:* **L'appétit vient en mangent,** *which means "Eating whets the appetite." I hope this volume awakens your appetite for tenderly prepared food—and for each other.*

Bon appétit!

# appetizers

*There is no better way to begin a special meal than with champagne oysters or a warm obster salad. These extravagant dishes will satiate your hunger, but they will ignite your appetite for lovemaking.*

# Grilled Fig Salad with Goat Cheese and Prosciutto

Yield: 2 servings

## figs

Plutarch, the Greek historian, biographer, and philosopher (A.D. 46–120), described the lively festival of Dionysia, at which figs were symbolically offered with drink and wine to the god, in addition to a goat and the all-important phallus. Figs represent both the female and male genitalia: the rich, rosy color and curvy shape evoke a woman's secrets, while the fig leaf provided a modest covering for men in Western sculpture and painting—leaving their secrets to the titillated imagination. Cut one in half lengthwise and scoop out the flesh with your tongue.

### Sherry Vinaigrette

2   tablespoons minced shallots
2   tablespoons sherry vinegar
6   tablespoons extra-virgin olive oil
    Salt and freshly ground black pepper to taste

In a small bowl, combine all the ingredients. Cover and set aside overnight to allow the flavors to mellow.

### Dried Fig Gremolata

3   dried figs, minced
2   tablespoons walnuts, toasted and finely ground
1   tablespoon chopped fresh parsley
    Zest of 1 orange, minced

In a small bowl, combine all the ingredients. Reserve.

### Salad

2   fresh Black Mission figs, halved
1   tablespoon extra-virgin olive oil
    Salt and freshly ground black pepper to taste
1   teaspoon fresh lemon juice
1   teaspoon freshly ground cardamom
4   thin slices prosciutto di Parma
½   pound/225g mesclun greens
    One 2-ounce/60g log aged goat cheese, cut into cubes
4   stalks chives

1. In a small bowl, toss the fresh fig halves with the olive oil. Season with salt and pepper. Grill lightly on both sides over a hot grill.

2. In another bowl, combine the lemon juice and cardamom. Add the grilled figs and toss until combined. Wrap each fig half in 1 slice prosciutto.

3. In a large bowl, combine the mesclun with the vinaigrette and toss to coat. Divide the salad between 2 salad plates. Place 2 prosciutto-wrapped figs on each plate. Garnish each salad with 1 ounce/30g goat cheese and 2 chives. Sprinkle the fig gremolata on top. Serve immediately.

## nuts

Although some people maintain that aphrodisiac foods are usually exotic and expensive, I find that many foods thought to arouse desire are readily available and affordable. Chestnuts and walnuts in England, pine nuts in New Mexico and Italy, and cashews in Brazil and India are some examples. The Arab writer Nefzawí recommended this bedtime snack for "he who feels weak for coition": a glass of honey, 20 almonds, and 100 pine nuts, repeated for three nights. Most nuts are high in fat, potassium, and phosphorus, as well as incomplete proteins and other nutrients; thus they have sustained humankind through times of dire scarcity. We now include them in dishes from pesto to pies, but nuts cracked open and shared on a crisp night are perhaps the most arousing.

# Mixed Green Salad with Toasted Walnuts and Tomato-Herb Vinaigrette

YIELD: 4 SERVINGS

2   *ripe medium tomatoes*
2   *tablespoons balsamic vinegar or lemon juice or a mixture of the two*
1   *teaspoon dried basil*
¼   *teaspoon dried thyme*
¼   *teaspoon dried tarragon*

*Salt and freshly ground black pepper to taste*
¼   *cup/60ml extra-virgin olive oil*
2   *tablespoons walnut halves*
4   *cups/200g assorted salad greens, such as endive, arugula, Bibb or Boston lettuce, and radicchio*

1. In a small saucepan, bring 2 cups/500ml water to a boil. Meanwhile, with a paring knife, cut out the stems from the tomatoes and make a small "X" in the opposite ends. Plunge the tomatoes in the boiling water and leave them in just until the skins are loosened, 10 to 20 seconds. With a slotted spoon, remove the tomatoes and rinse them under cold water until cool enough to handle. Slip off the skins and cut the tomatoes in half. Gently but firmly squeeze the seeds from the tomato halves. Chop coarsely.

2. In a blender, combine the chopped tomatoes, vinegar or lemon juice, basil, thyme, and tarragon. Season with salt and pepper. Blend at high speed until the mixture is smooth. Reduce the speed to low and slowly add the oil in a steady stream, continuing to blend until the oil is fully incorporated and the dressing is smooth. Let stand at room temperature to allow the flavors to mellow, about 30 minutes.

3. Meanwhile, toast the walnuts: In a dry skillet over high heat, toss or stir the walnuts, taking care not to scorch them, until lightly browned.

4. In a salad bowl, toss the salad greens with just enough dressing to lightly coat the leaves. Add the toasted walnut halves and toss again briefly. Serve immediately.

# Portobello Mushroom Salad with Roasted Red Pepper Vinaigrette

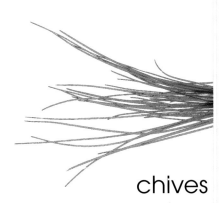

## chives

The thin, tubular leaves of this bulb plant taste softly reminiscent of the onions to which it is related. The delicate flavor indicates a less powerful aphrodisiac than that of onions—and sometimes subtlety is the best strategy when cooking for a tired, overworked lover. Try chives in egg and cheese dishes, and slip them into soups for a sultry starter.

### Roasted Red Pepper Vinaigrette

1 red bell pepper
½ teaspoon Dijon mustard
1 teaspoon sherry vinegar
3 teaspoons peanut oil

1. Place the bell pepper directly over the flame of a gas stove or under the broiler. Roast, turning frequently, until the skin is blackened on all sides. Remove, place in a bowl, and cover for 2 minutes.

2. Remove and discard the skin, seeds, and core from the bell pepper. Place in a blender with the mustard, vinegar, and oil. Puree until smooth. Reserve.

### Mushroom Salad

2 teaspoons balsamic vinegar
1 teaspoon chopped garlic
3 teaspoons extra-virgin olive oil
2 portobello mushrooms, 6 inches/15cm in diameter
2 yellow Roma tomatoes
  Salt and freshly ground black pepper to taste
2 ounces/60g mixed baby greens
½ tablespoon chopped fresh chives

1. Heat a charcoal grill or broiler. In a small bowl, whisk the balsamic vinegar, garlic, and olive oil. Brush some of this marinade on the mushrooms and grill until well marked, about 4 minutes. Set aside and keep warm.

2. Meanwhile, cut the top quarter off the tomatoes. Scrape out the seeds and let the tomatoes drain. Season with salt and pepper.

3. In a medium bowl, toss the greens with enough of the remaining marinade to coat lightly. Place greens in each tomato, like a bouquet into a vase. Place each tomato on a plate. Slice the mushrooms on the diagonal and fan onto each plate. Drizzle the mushrooms with the roasted bell pepper vinaigrette and sprinkle with the chives.

# Marinated Tomato Salad with Garlic Croutons

YIELD: 2 SERVINGS

### Garlic Croutons

2 tablespoons olive oil
4 cloves garlic, crushed
1 cup/60g cubed crustless sourdough bread

In a medium skillet, heat the olive oil over medium heat. Add the garlic cloves and cook, stirring, until golden. Remove from the heat and discard the garlic. Add the bread cubes to the skillet and toss to coat. Return to the heat and cook, tossing continually, until toasted and golden. Transfer to a plate lined with paper towels to drain. Reserve.

### Tomato Salad

½ medium cucumber, peeled
½ medium red onion, thinly sliced
4 tablespoons olive oil
½ tablespoon chopped fresh oregano
Salt and freshly ground black pepper to taste
1 large red tomato, cored and cut into 1-inch/2.5cm chunks
1 large yellow tomato, cored and cut into 1-inch/2.5cm chunks
7 fresh basil leaves, torn in half
6 fresh parsley leaves, chopped coarsely
1 teaspoon finely chopped garlic
2 ounces feta cheese, broken into bite-size pieces
2 teaspoons red wine vinegar
10 Niçoise olives, pitted

1. Quarter each cucumber lengthwise, then cut each quarter into thin crosswise slices. Transfer to a bowl. Add the onion, 2 tablespoons olive oil, and the oregano. Toss to coat thoroughly with the oil. Season with salt and pepper. Let marinate for 15 minutes.

2. In a large nonreactive bowl, combine the tomatoes, remaining 2 tablespoons olive oil, basil, parsley, and garlic. Toss to coat thoroughly with the oil. Season with salt and pepper. Let marinate for 5 minutes.

3. To serve, add the cucumber mixture, feta, and vinegar to the tomato mixture. Toss until well combined. Divide the salad between 2 large salad bowls and sprinkle with the croutons. Scatter the olives over the salads and serve immediately.

## salt

As Aphrodite rose from the sea, the ancient Greeks believed that all life originated there—centuries before the theory of evolution. As proof of our marine origins, our bodily fluids contain salt in about the same proportion as is found in seawater. Salt is essential to life itself; it transmits nerve impulses and regulates muscle contractions; we die without it. At one time salt was more precious than gold to the Europeans, who were convinced it was an aphrodisiac through at least the Middle Ages. Salt preserves food, brightens and balances its flavors, and heightens the experience of eating. And for some couples, that is reason enough to embrace it.

# Arugula Salad with Jalapeño Vinegar

YIELD: 4 SERVINGS

### Jalapeño Vinegar

3 cups/750ml white wine vinegar
4 jalapeño peppers or serrano chiles

In a 1-quart/1 liter jar with a tight-fitting lid, combine the vinegar and peppers. Let stand at room temperature for 3 to 4 weeks before using.

### Arugula Salad

¼ cup/60ml extra-virgin olive oil
1 tablespoon whole black peppercorns
4 bunches arugula, washed in cold water, drained, and dried

In a large salad bowl, combine the olive oil, 2 tablespoons jalapeño vinegar, and the peppercorns. Just before serving, add the arugula and toss.

## arugula

Horace, the first-century Roman poet and satirist, wrote of arugula's piquant bite, and his countrymen agreed that it strengthened their members. Once found mainly in Italian restaurants, frizzy arugula now sprouts up in supermarkets and grows abundantly in backyard gardens, where it is easily accessible to the adventurous gourmets who add its tongue-shaped leaves to their stimulating salads.

# Shaved Fennel and Frisée Salad with Lemon Vinaigrette

YIELD: 2 SERVINGS

### Lemon Vinaigrette

1 teaspoon minced shallot
1 tablespoon champagne vinegar
4 tablespoons fresh lemon juice
¼ cup/60ml extra-virgin olive oil
2 tablespoons olive oil
Salt and freshly ground black pepper to taste

In a mixing bowl, combine the shallot, vinegar, and 2 tablespoons lemon juice. Slowly whisk in the olive oils. Season to taste with remaining lemon juice, salt, and pepper.

### Salad

1 head frisée or chicory
1 bulb fennel
½ shallot, minced
¼ bunch fresh chives, chopped
Fresh pecorino cheese for garnish

Remove and discard any dark green, bitter leaves from the frisée. Rinse and place in a bowl. Using a mandoline or the long, sharp blade on a grater, thinly shave the fennel bulbs and combine with the frisée. Add the shallot and chives and toss with the vinaigrette. Shave pecorino cheese over the top. Serve immediately.

Arugula Salad
with Jalapeño Vinegar

# Warm Lobster Salad on Baby Lettuce

YIELD: 2 SERVINGS

One 1 ½-pound/680g lobster
¼ cucumber, peeled, halved lengthwise, seeded, and cut into half moons
6 spears pencil asparagus
1 ripe medium tomato
6 tablespoons/90g unsalted butter
4 large white mushrooms, thinly sliced

Salt and freshly ground black pepper to taste
Juice of ½ lemon
1 tablespoon port wine
2 ounces/60g mixed baby lettuces or mesclun
1 tablespoon chopped fresh chervil
Red peppercorns for garnish

1. In a stockpot, bring 1 gallon/4 liters salted water to a boil over high heat. Place the lobster in the pot head first so that it is completely submerged. Cover the pot and return to a boil. Boil for 6 minutes and remove from the pot. Remove the claw and tail. Slice the tail meat into even chunks and reserve with the claws. Split the head and carcass and reserve with the legs as a garnish.

2. In a medium saucepan, bring 2 quarts/2 liters salted water to a boil over high heat. Add the cucumber and cook until tender, about 2 minutes. With a slotted spoon or strainer, remove the cucumber strips, transfer them to a small bowl, and reserve. Add the asparagus to the boiling water and repeat the process of cooking, removing with a slotted spoon and transferring to a bowl after approximately 2 minutes.

3. While that same pan of water is boiling, with a paring knife, cut out the stem from the tomato and make a small "X" in the opposite end. Plunge the tomato in the boiling water and leave it in just until the skin is loosened, 10 to 20 seconds. With a slotted spoon, remove the tomato and rinse under cold water until cool enough to handle. Slip off the skin and cut the tomato in half. Gently but firmly squeeze the seeds from the tomato halves. Dice the tomato. Reserve.

4. Sauté the lobster meat, cucumber, asparagus, and tomato lightly in 1 tablespoon butter for 1 minute. On the top of each plate arrange 3 or 4 cucumber strips, 3 asparagus spears, the slices of 1 mushroom, and 1 tablespoon diced tomato. On the bottom half of each plate, place some lobster medallions and a lobster claw. Season all components with salt and pepper. Place the plate in a low oven briefly to warm and brush everything with melted butter.

5. Meanwhile, in a skillet, heat 2 tablespoons butter over medium heat. Add the lemon juice and cook, stirring, just until heated through, 1 to 2 minutes. Add the port and cook, stirring, until reduced by half. Whisk in the remaining butter and season with salt and pepper. Reserve.

6. To serve, place a handful of baby lettuce in the center of each plate and spoon the lemon sauce over the lobster salads. Top with the warmed lobster heads and legs and diced tomatoes. Garnish with the chervil and red peppercorns.

# Lobster Salad with Mango-Mint Chutney

YIELD: 2 SERVINGS

One 1 ½- to 2-pound/680 to 900g lobster, cooked, shelled, chilled, and cut into ½-inch/ 1.25cm chunks (about ½ pound/225g lobster meat)

8   medium Boston lettuce leaves, washed in cold water and drained

2   canned artichoke hearts

½   cup/125ml mango-mint chutney (recipe follows)

Divide the lettuce between 2 plates. Place an artichoke heart in the center of each plate and top with the lobster meat. Garnish with the chutney and serve.

## mint

Perhaps no other herb smells, tastes, and feels so refreshing as mint in its many varieties, including the familiar peppermint and spearmint. Middle Easterners and Europeans have documented its libido-enhancing properties and incorporated it into everything from lamb and tabbouleh to tea and ice cream. Americans even use it in soaps and toothpaste. Fortunately, mint is easy to grow just outside your back door, where you can fondle its veined leaves to release their invigorating scent. Toss a handful in your bathwater, light a candle, and leave the door ajar.

### Mango-Mint Chutney

YIELD: 1 QUART/1 LITER

3   tablespoons cider vinegar, plus extra as needed

½   small red onion, finely chopped
    Grated zest and juice of 1 large orange
    Grated zest and juice of 2 small lemons

2   teaspoons grated fresh ginger

1   stick cinnamon

½   cup/60g raisins

2   cloves
    Pinch freshly grated nutmeg
    Pinch ground coriander, toasted

3   large mangoes, peeled, pitted, and cut into medium dice

1 ½ tablespoons light brown sugar, plus extra as needed

2   teaspoons chopped fresh mint

In a medium nonreactive saucepan, combine all the ingredients except the mangoes, brown sugar, and mint. Cook slowly over low heat, stirring occasionally, until almost dry. Add the mangoes and the sugar. Add more vinegar or brown sugar to taste.

When the mangoes are heated through, remove from the heat and let cool. Stir in the chopped mint and transfer to a bowl. Cover and refrigerate until ready to use.

# Guacamole

YIELD: 2 CUPS/500ML

2 medium tomatoes, seeded and finely diced
1 small onion, finely diced
2 serrano chiles, halved, seeded, and finely chopped
2 tablespoons chopped fresh cilantro
2 ripe Haas avocados
½ teaspoon salt
   Freshly ground black pepper to taste
1 tablespoon fresh lime juice

In a medium bowl, combine the tomatoes, onion, chiles, and cilantro. Peel the avocados and add the flesh to the bowl. With a fork, crush the avocado and mix well, still keeping a chunky consistency. Add the salt, freshly ground black pepper to taste, and lime juice. Serve on slices of avocado with corn chips.

## avocados

This fruit echoes the soft curves of a woman yet is also reminiscent of a man's nether regions; the Aztecs called it *ahuacatl*, meaning "testicle." Florida avocados are large, bright green, and shiny; California (Haas) ones are small, dark, and warty looking—and by far the better of the two. At the market, pick up one of these "alligator pears" and feel its bumpy skin, noticing its relative weight. Apply gentle pressure with the whole hand, for avocados are sensitive to too much poking. Allow your new friend to ripen at room temperature, then cut in half lengthwise right before your tête-à-tête. Twist to split the two halves, manipulate the spherical seed with a rocking motion to pry it loose, and sprinkle the creamy insides with citrus juice to prevent browning. True avocado aficionados rush to scoop out the green, buttery fruit with a spoon; those who manage to restrain themselves slice it or spoon salads into the hollow where the seed once nestled.

The good news is that avocados are high in vitamins A and C, niacin, and minerals, including phosphorus and potassium. The bright side of the bad news is that these fruits are also high in fat, so it is to your advantage to split one with your lover.

# Baked Carrot and Zucchini Cakes

YIELD: 8 SERVINGS

1 ½ cups/120g grated carrots
1 ½ cups/120g grated zucchini
1 ½ cups/180g dried currants
5 large eggs, lightly beaten
1 cup/250ml vegetable oil
2 teaspoons pure vanilla extract

2 ¾ cups/220g all-purpose flour
1 tablespoon baking soda
½ teaspoon ground cinnamon
1 ¼ cups/285g sugar
½ teaspoon salt
⅓ cup/50g poppy seeds

1. Preheat the oven to 375°F/190°C. Coat a 13-by-9-inch/33-by-23cm baking dish with butter. Dust the dish with a little flour, tilting it to coat evenly and tapping out the excess.

2. Place the carrots in a clean kitchen towel and squeeze to remove excess moisture. Transfer the carrots to a bowl. Repeat the process with the zucchini. Add the currants and set aside.

3. In a medium bowl, whisk the eggs, oil, and vanilla until well blended. In a large bowl, combine the flour, baking soda, cinnamon, sugar, salt, and poppy seeds. Make a well in the center of the dry ingredients. Add the wet ingredients and stir until just combined.

4. With a rubber spatula, fold the vegetables and currants into the batter until just combined. Pour the batter into the prepared baking dish and bake for 40 minutes, or until a skewer inserted in the center comes out clean. Transfer the baking dish to a wire rack and let cool completely, about 1 hour, before serving.

# Blinis and Caviar

YIELD: 4 SERVINGS

9 tablespoons/135g unsalted butter
2 cups/500ml whole milk
½ tablespoon active dry yeast
2 teaspoons sugar
3 cups/360g all-purpose flour

3 large eggs, separated
½ teaspoon salt
One 4-ounce/120g tin beluga, osetra, or sevruga caviar

1. Melt the butter in a medium saucepan over low heat. Measure out 5 tablespoons/75g and set aside. Cook the remaining butter until the butterfat becomes clear and the milk solids drop to the bottom of the pan. Skim the surface foam as the butter separates. Carefully ladle the clear butterfat into another bowl and reserve. Discard the milky liquid at the bottom of the saucepan.

2. In another heavy medium saucepan, bring the milk to a boil over medium heat. Remove from the heat and let cool. When the milk is lukewarm, add the yeast; stir until dissolved. With a wooden spoon, slowly blend in the sugar and 1 cup/120g flour. Cover the pan with a damp kitchen towel and set in a warm place (75°F/24°C) until the mixture is doubled in volume, about 2 hours.

3. In a medium mixing bowl, combine the egg yolks, 5 tablespoons melted butter, and salt. With an electric mixer, beat at medium speed until completely smooth, stopping 2 or 3 times to scrape down the sides of the bowl. Add the egg mixture and remaining flour to the yeast mixture and stir until combined. Replace the damp towel and once again set in a warm place until the mixture is doubled in volume, about 1 hour.

4. Place the egg whites in a clean, grease-free mixing bowl. With an electric mixer, beat at low speed until frothy. Increase the speed to medium-high and beat until the whites hold stiff, but not dry, peaks. With a rubber spatula, fold the egg whites into the yeast batter. Let stand for 10 minutes.

5. Place a large skillet over medium-high heat. With a pastry brush, coat the pan with some of the clarified butter. Drop 4 spoonfuls of batter into the skillet. When golden on the bottom, flip the blinis and cook for just a few seconds more. Divide the blinis among 4 warmed plates. Repeat with the remaining batter.

6. To serve, top the blinis with spoonfuls of caviar. Serve immediately.

## ghee
### (Clarified Butter)

Long before our concerns about cholesterol and saturated fat, Indians drank ghee, or clarified butter, in the morning to promote health and strength. Ghee is the base of many concoctions prescribed in the *Kama Sutra*. The author blends it with sexy substances such as honey and jasmine flowers.
If you find the slippery sweetness of clarified butter to be a turn-on, experiment by dipping a few asparagus stalks or artichoke leaves (or your lover's fingers) in it. Indulge with restraint, for you'll want to stay fit and healthy enough to enjoy him or her to the fullest.

# Champagne Oysters with Potato Cakes

Yield: 2 servings

## Potato Cakes

2   large russet potatoes
½   large onion
1   tablespoon fresh lemon juice
1   large egg, lightly beaten

1   tablespoon chopped fresh parsley
    Salt and freshly ground black pepper to taste
2   tablespoons vegetable oil

1. Grate the potatoes and finely chop the onion. Combine and toss with lemon juice to prevent discoloration.

2. Preheat the oven to 200°F/95°C and place a baking sheet in it. Place the potato and onion mixture in a clean kitchen towel and squeeze dry. Transfer to a small bowl and add the egg and parsley. Season with salt and pepper. Using the palms of your hands, form the mixture into 2 patties.

3. In a large skillet, heat the oil over medium heat. Add the potato cakes. With a metal spatula, press down on each potato cake until it is flat and even all the way around. Sauté the potato cakes until golden, about 3 minutes per side. Transfer to the baking sheet in the oven to keep warm while cooking the oysters.

## Champagne Oysters

½    cup/125ml champagne
1½   tablespoons finely chopped shallots
¾    cup/200ml heavy cream
4    tablespoons/60g unsalted butter, softened
12   oysters, freshly shucked

1    tablespoon chopped fresh thyme
     Salt and freshly ground black pepper to taste
1    ounce/30g black or Russian caviar
2    tablespoons chopped fresh chives

1. In a wide medium saucepan, combine the champagne and shallots over medium heat. Simmer until the liquid is reduced by half. Slowly add the cream, whisking constantly. Return to a simmer and reduce by one-fourth. Add the butter, a tablespoon/15g at a time, whisking until thickened; be careful not to let the mixture overheat or the butter will separate.

2. Add the oysters to the sauce and simmer gently just until the oysters are firm. Add the thyme. Season with salt and pepper.

3. To serve, divide the potato cakes between 2 warmed plates. Spoon 6 oysters on each cake. Drizzle some sauce over the oysters, top with caviar, and sprinkle with chives. Serve immediately.

## potatoes

Spanish explorers discovered these "testicles of the earth" in Peru, then brought them back to Europe, where people dismissed them as either a poison or an aphrodisiac (or both). The Spaniards later brought them to Ireland, where the starving masses found the lowly potato to be a sustaining godsend. The English associated the potato with their lusty, singing, dancing neighbors across the Irish Sea, and no doubt blamed the vegetable for the notorious Irish birthrate. Shakespeare, who was more than aware of theatergoers' fascination with aphrodisiacs, referred to potatoes in *The Merry Wives of Windsor*: "Let the sky rain potatoes/kissing comfits and snow eryngoes."

# Belgian Endive Canapés with Caviar

2 cups/500ml heavy cream
1 ½ cups/375ml sour cream

12 Belgian endive leaves or ⅛-inch/3mm slices
    of cucumber
6 ounces/180g Russian caviar

1. To make crème frâiche, heat the heavy cream over low heat in a small saucepan, stirring continuously, for approximately 6 minutes, until just lukewarm. Do not boil. Remove from the heat. Alternatively, you may use store-bought crème frâiche.

2. In a medium mixing bowl, whisk the sour cream until smooth, approximately 2 minutes. Add the lukewarm heavy cream to the sour cream and whisk until well combined. Cover with a clean kitchen towel and let stand at room temperature for 15 hours, or until thick.

3. Transfer the mixture to a container; cover and refrigerate overnight. (The crème fraîche will keep, covered, in the refrigerator for up to 10 days.)

4. To make the canapés, place a small dollop of crème fraîche at the root end of each endive leaf. Scoop some caviar on each dollop of crème fraîche and serve immediately.

## roe

Caviar is the queen of fish eggs, but other types of roe add variety and cost less. Europeans swear by cod and herring roe; the Japanese love their orange-red salmon and flying fish roe. Sea urchin—*uni* to all you sushi-bar enthusiasts—is sought after for its creamy orange roe. The ovaries are served on vinegared rice in Japan and on crusty bread in the Caribbean. A Filipino friend recently blessed with his firstborn assures me, "It was the *uni*."

# Scallop Canapés with Caviar

12 toasted 1-inch/2.5cm rounds of white bread,
    thinly spread with butter or mayonnaise
12 cooked scallops
    Frisée leaves for garnish
12 teaspoons Russian or salmon caviar

Cover the toasted bread rounds with the scallops. Garnish with frisée and top with caviar.

# Caviar and Celery Canapés

YIELD: 12 CANAPÉS

## celery

The ancient Greeks and Romans documented the medicinal virtues of celery. Since then, everyone from the Haitians to the Chinese has associated the firm, light green stalks with their suggestive magic. Cream of celery soup quickened French pulses during the eighteenth century, as the mistress of Louis XV, Madame de Pompadour (1721–64) attested, and the soup remains a favorite in France today. Crunch on a chilled stick while stirring at the stove; you'll immediately feel its cool jolt.

1 pound/454g cream cheese
3 tablespoons sour cream
2 tablespoons chopped fresh chives

3 stalks celery, washed, peeled, and cut into twelve 3-inch/7.5cm sticks
6 ounces/180g black or Russian caviar

1. Place the cream cheese in a medium mixing bowl. With an electric mixer, beat at medium speed until light and fluffy. Add the sour cream and chives. Beat until well blended.

2. Using a pastry bag fitted with a medium star tip or a resealable bag clipped at one of the corners, pipe the cream cheese mixture in the cavity of each celery stalk. Top with the caviar and serve immediately.

# Smoked Cod Roe Canapé

YIELD: 12 CANAPÉS

3 slices good-quality white bread, toasted and buttered, crusts trimmed, and cut into quarters
6 ounces/180g smoked cod roe
6 tablespoons crème fraîche (page 16)
Juice of 1 lemon
Freshly ground black pepper to taste
12 sprigs dill

Arrange the toast points on a serving platter. Spread a thin layer of smoked cod roe on each one. Top with a dollop of crème fraîche. Sprinkle lemon juice and pepper over each canapé and garnish with a sprig of dill. Serve immediately.

# Smoked Salmon Canapés

YIELD: 12 CANAPÉS

12   *thinly sliced pieces smoked salmon,*
    *1 ½ inches/4cm wide*
12   *toasted 1-inch/2.5cm rounds of white bread,*
    *thinly spread with butter or mayonnaise*
    *Dill sprigs for garnish*
12   *teaspoons Russian caviar (optional)*

Create a rose by rolling each piece of smoked salmon and perch on top of a toast circle. Garnish with a dill sprig and caviar if desired.

# Caviar and Artichoke Canapés

YIELD: 12 CANAPÉS

12   *small to medium artichokes or canned*
    *artichoke bottoms*
3   *tablespoons all-purpose flour*

  *Juice of 1 lemon*
6   *tablespoons sour cream*
6   *ounces/180g black or Russian caviar*

1. If using canned artichokes, skip to step 4. Otherwise, twist the stems off the artichokes and snap off the outside leaves. Leave the bunch of yellowish leaves in the center intact.

2. In a small bowl, combine the flour with enough water to make a saucelike consistency. Fill a large pot with 1 gallon/4 liters water, stir in the flour mixture, and whisk to combine. Add the lemon juice and bring to a boil over medium heat.

3. Add the artichokes to the pot and boil until you can easily pierce the bottoms with a knife, about 20 minutes. (The larger the artichokes, the more time it will take to cook them.) Drain upside down in a colander and remove the leaves and hairy choke. Refresh in a large bowl of ice water and let cool for 10 minutes. Drain on paper towels.

4. Arrange the artichoke bottoms on a serving plate. Top each one with a dollop of sour cream and some caviar. Serve immediately.

## artichokes

Catherine de Médicis (1519–89) is credited for bringing these prickly thistles to France from their native Sicily or from northern Africa. They are at their best in the spring—Aphrodite's favorite season. Some food lovers find the artichoke's thorny exterior hard to resist. The leaves and heart have been attributed with many powers, from restoring health to inducing euphoria. When you dip the fleshy leaves into clarified butter or a delicate vinaigrette, you will understand the cry of Parisian street vendors translated below:
*Artichokes! Artichokes!*
*Heats the body and the spirit.*
*Heats the genitals!*

# Foie Gras with Figs and Mixed Greens

YIELD: 2 SERVINGS

*Two 5-ounce/150g slices grade B fresh foie gras*
*3  fresh figs, 1 cut into quarters, 2 sliced*
*1  shallot, coarsely chopped*
*Freshly ground black pepper to taste*
*2  tablespoons port wine*
*2  tablespoons red wine*

*2  tablespoons veal or chicken stock*
*Salt to taste*
*¼  pound/120g mixed baby greens*
*Lemon vinaigrette (page 8)*
*2  sprigs chervil*

1. Trim the ends off the foie gras and reserve the slices and trimmings. Preheat the oven to 350°F/180°C.

2. In a medium saucepan, heat the foie gras trimmings until the fat is rendered, about 2 minutes. Add the fig quarters and shallot to the saucepan; cook until slightly caramelized, about 4 minutes. Season with black pepper. Add the port and red wine and reduce until the liquid is almost evaporated.

3. Add the stock and reduce until the sauce coats the back of a spoon, about 8 minutes. Strain through a fine sieve into a small saucepan and discard the fig quarters. Season with salt and more pepper if needed.

4. Meanwhile, heat a large, heavy, ovenproof pan or cast-iron skillet over high heat until just smoking. Add the foie gras slices and sear until colored on both sides, 2 to 3 minutes per side. Add the fig slices and sauté until tender. Place in the oven to finish the cooking, no longer than 4 minutes.

5. To serve, toss the baby greens with lemon vinaigrette until just coated. Season with salt and pepper. Place the greens at the top of each plate. Lay some fig slices at the bottom of the plate. Surround with sauce and top with the foie gras. Garnish with chervil sprigs and serve immediately.

# truffles

These fungi, which grow several inches underground near the roots of certain hardwood trees, are potent aphrodisiacs. The ancient Romans adored truffles, for which they traded gold and jewels. These scarce lumps refuse to be cultivated and thrive in precious few locales and only during certain months. White truffles, at their strong, earthy best in the Piedmont region of northern Italy, are believed to produce a sexually attractive scent like that released by male mammals. Black truffles, sometimes compared to porcini, hazelnuts, and oysters, are the pride of the Périgord region of southwestern France. George IV of England (1762–1830) was enamored of Italian truffles, while Louis XIV (1638–1715), Napoleon Bonaparte (1769–1821), and novelist Honoré de Balzac (1799–1850) favored those of France. Those who unearth and sell truffles train pigs and dogs to scent them out and shroud their transactions in mystery, carefully guarding the secret hiding places of this sensual buried treasure.

# Baked Potatoes with Truffles and Caviar

Yield: 2 servings

2 large baking potatoes, such as russet
6 tablespoons/90g unsalted butter
¼ cup/60ml olive oil

2 medium white truffles, 1 chopped, 1 left whole
Salt and freshly ground black pepper to taste
2 tablespoons black or Russian caviar

1. Preheat the oven to 400°F/200°C. Scrub the potatoes under cold running water and dry thoroughly with paper towels. Prick all over with a fork and bake for 45 minutes, or until cooked through.

2. Transfer the potatoes to a cutting board and cut a thin horizontal slice off each one. Scoop the pulp of the potatoes into a medium bowl, keeping the skins intact. Using a fork, crush the pulp with 4 tablespoons/60g butter, the olive oil, and the chopped truffle. Season with salt and pepper. Stuff the mashed potatoes back into the potato skins and return to the oven for 10 minutes, or until reheated.

3. To serve, melt the remaining 2 tablespoons/30g butter in a small saucepan over medium heat. Place each stuffed potato on a plate. Drizzle the hot butter over the potatoes, shave a few thin slices of truffle on top, and garnish with a tablespoon of caviar. Serve immediately.

# Vidalia Onion Tart

YIELD: 8 SERVINGS

## Tart Shell

1  cup/120g all-purpose flour
   Pinch salt
1  stick plus 2 tablespoons/150g unsalted butter,
   cut into small pieces

2  tablespoons ice water
1  large egg, beaten

1. In a large bowl, combine the flour and salt. Using your fingertips, work the butter into the flour until the mixture resembles coarse meal. Add the water and egg, stirring with a fork until the mixture forms a dough. Pat into a cylinder and chill, covered with plastic wrap, for at least 1 hour or up to 3 days.

2. Preheat the oven to 400°F/200°C. On a lightly floured surface, roll out the dough into an 11-inch/28cm round. Drape the dough over a rolling pin and fit it into a 9-inch/23cm pie pan. Fold the edges under and crimp. Prick the shell all over with the tines of a fork to prevent bubbling during baking.

3. Place a piece of aluminum foil over the dough and fill it with pie weights or beans. Place the shell in the oven and bake for 25 minutes, or until lightly golden. Remove from the oven, place on a wire rack, and let cool.

## Filling

2    tablespoons/30g unsalted butter
¼    cup/30g diced slab bacon
6 to 8  Vidalia onions, sliced (about 4 cups)
1¼   cups/310ml heavy cream
1    cup/250ml whole milk

4  large eggs
2  tablespoons Calvados
2  tablespoons finely chopped parsley stems
   Salt and freshly ground black pepper to taste
   Freshly ground nutmeg to taste

1. In a nonstick skillet, melt the butter over medium heat. Add the bacon and cook until softened and golden brown, 6 minutes. Add the onion slices and sauté until softened, 4 minutes. Remove from the heat and let cool.

2. Preheat the oven to 400°F/200°C. In a large bowl, whisk the cream, milk, eggs, and Calvados. Add the onion mixture and the parsley stems. Season with salt, pepper, and nutmeg. Pour the egg mixture into the baked tart shell.

3. Place the tart in the oven and immediately reduce the temperature to 350°F/180°C. Bake for 30 minutes. Turn the oven off and bake for 20 minutes more. Cut into wedges to serve. Leftovers may be served cold or may be frozen and reheated.

# Chilled Asparagus with Vinaigrette Dressing

1  pound/454g asparagus
½  clove garlic, minced
1  shallot, diced
   Juice of ½ lemon
½  tablespoon sherry vinegar
½  teaspoon Dijon mustard

3  tablespoons olive oil
2  tablespoons walnut oil
   Salt and freshly ground black pepper to taste
1  red bell pepper, cored, seeded, and cut
   into julienne strips
1  heart of palm, cut into rounds

## asparagus

A fine, firm phallic symbol, this member of the lily family is esteemed worldwide for its aphrodisiac nature. The Chinese used asparagus to treat infertility as early as 200 B.C., and its evocative effect did not escape the notice of ancient Arabs and Romans. Perhaps they linked the cultivation of their own romantic love—and the resulting tendency to multiply—with this plant's exuberant growth. Some well-tended stalks can grow up to 10 inches/25cm a day, and gardening zealots may find themselves harvesting twice daily in the spring. As in all matters of love, patience is rewarded in the long run: resist cutting your asparagus stalks for the first three years, and the plants will produce this invigorating delicacy for up to two decades. The green, white, and violet varieties all contain asparagine, a nutrient essential for prostate health.

1. Bring a large saucepan of salted water to a boil. Prepare a large bowl of ice water. Pare down the base of any large asparagus spears with a vegetable peeler to remove any fibrous outer layer. Place the asparagus in the boiling water and cook until just tender but still bright green, 3 to 5 minutes. Drain immediately and shock in the ice water for 5 minutes to stop the cooking.

2. Meanwhile, in a blender or food processor, puree the garlic, shallot, lemon juice, vinegar, and mustard. With the motor running, slowly add the olive oil and walnut oil through the feed tube. Strain through a fine sieve into a nonreactive bowl. Season with salt and pepper.

3. Drain the asparagus and dry on paper towels. Arrange on a platter along with the red pepper and the heart of palm. Drizzle with the vinaigrette and serve immediately.

# Seafood Platter
# with Oyster Mayonnaise

YIELD: 2 SERVINGS

8 large oysters, scrubbed well under cold water

6 jumbo shrimp, cooked, peeled,
  and deveined

1 small head Belgian endive

2 crisp lettuce leaves

4 sprigs dill

½ large red, green, or yellow bell pepper,
  cored, seeded, and diced

2 crayfish, cooked (optional)

1 medium lemon, sliced
  Oyster mayonnaise (recipe follows)

Using an oyster knife, open the oysters but leave them in the shell. Loosen the oysters around the edges for easier eating. Arrange a bed of crushed ice on a serving platter and place the oysters and the shrimp on the ice. Garnish the plate with the endive leaves, lettuce, dill, and diced bell pepper. In the center, place the 2 whole crayfish if using and the lemon slices. Serve with oyster mayonnaise in a separate dish for dipping.

## Oyster Mayonnaise

YIELD: 1 ½ TO 2 CUPS/375 TO 500 ML

1 tablespoon/15g unsalted butter

2½ tablespoons minced onion

1 tablespoon minced celery

1 bay leaf

½ teaspoon salt

½ teaspoon dry mustard

½ teaspoon cayenne pepper

¼ teaspoon freshly ground white pepper

¼ teaspoon dried basil

⅛ teaspoon dried thyme

  Pinch dried oregano

3 oysters, freshly shucked

1 large egg

1¼ cups/310ml olive oil

1 tablespoon white wine vinegar

½ teaspoon Tabasco sauce

1. In a medium skillet, melt the butter over medium heat. Add the onion, celery, bay leaf, and salt. Cook, stirring, until the onion softens. Add the mustard, cayenne, white pepper, basil, thyme, and oregano. Stir well to combine.

2. Add the oysters and sauté quickly until just cooked. Transfer the contents of the skillet to the bowl of a food processor. Let cool, then puree the oysters until smooth.

3. With the motor running, add the egg, then very, very slowly add the olive oil, stopping once or twice to scrape down the sides. The mixture should become very thick. Season with the vinegar and Tabasco. Transfer to a small nonreactive bowl, cover, and chill in the refrigerator until ready to serve with the seafood platter. This can also be used to accompany any fried fish.

# Fried Calamari with Spicy Anchovy Mayonnaise

Yield: 4 servings

### Anchovy Mayonnaise

½   cup/125ml prepared mayonnaise
6 to 8   anchovy fillets
2   tablespoons chopped fresh parsley
1   teaspoon fresh lemon juice
½   teaspoon cayenne pepper

In a food processor, puree all the ingredients until smooth. Divide among 4 individual ramekins.

### Calamari

½   pound/225g fresh or frozen small squid, cleaned (ink sac, cartilage, heads, and dark skin removed)
1½   quarts/3l peanut or light olive oil
⅓   cup/40g all-purpose flour
⅓   cup/50g graham cracker crumbs

Pinch ground cardamom
Salt to taste
4   lemon wedges
4   Belgian endive leaves (optional)

1. Slice the squid into rings no wider than ¼ inch/6mm. If the tentacles are large, halve or quarter them lengthwise.

2. In a deep, heavy saucepan, heat the oil to 350°F/180°C. (A small piece of bread dropped into the oil should float up to the surface almost immediately and brown within 45 seconds.)

3. Meanwhile, in a small bowl, combine the flour, graham cracker crumbs, and cardamom. Dredge the squid in this mixture and then toss in a mesh strainer to shake off any excess coating. Deep-fry the squid in batches until golden brown, about 2 minutes. Drain on paper towels and lightly salt. Serve immediately with the anchovy mayonnaise, lemon wedges, and, if desired, a garnish of Belgian endive leaves.

# Gravlax with Mustard-Dill Sauce

Y I E L D :   6   S E R V I N G S

## dill

In sixteenth- and seventeenth-century England, the seeds of this feathery herb were believed to arouse lust, and today some herbalists still steep the seeds in boiling water for that very purpose. However, it is probably more stimulating—to the eyes and the taste buds—to sprinkle the delightful green weed over aphrodisiac vegetables such as carrots, beets, and cabbage. Surely the Germans, Scandinavians, and Eastern Europeans could not all be wrong.

### Gravlax

1 pound/454g salmon fillet with skin, cut into 2 pieces
3 tablespoons salt
3 tablespoons sugar

2 tablespoons freshly ground white pepper
1 large bunch fresh dill, chopped

1. Remove the backbone and small bones from the salmon halves. Rinse and pat dry.

2. In a small bowl, combine the salt, sugar, and pepper. Rub all surfaces of the salmon with the mixture. Place 1 piece, skin side down, in a flat glass dish.

Spread half the dill over the salmon and cover with the second piece, skin side up. Sprinkle the remaining dill over the salmon and cover tightly with aluminum foil. Refrigerate for 4 days, turning the salmon every 24 hours. Drain the drippings.

### Mustard-Dill Sauce

¼ cup/60g sugar
¾ cup/200ml Dijon mustard
3 tablespoons white wine vinegar
1½ cups/375ml oil
Salt and freshly ground black pepper to taste
2 tablespoons finely chopped fresh dill

In a small nonreactive bowl, combine the sugar and the mustard. Whisk in the vinegar. Add the oil slowly, whisking constantly, until the sauce is thickened and creamy. Season with salt and pepper. Stir in the chopped dill.

### To Assemble

8 spears asparagus, fibrous ends removed
1 lemon, cut into wedges
4 sprigs dill

1. For the garnish, bring a medium saucepan of salted water to a boil. Add the asparagus and cook until tender. With a slotted spoon, remove the asparagus and plunge it into a bowl of cold water. Drain and reserve.

2. To serve, scrape the seasonings off the salmon and pat the fillets dry with a paper towel. Place the salmon, skin side down, on a cutting board. Using a sharp, thin, flexible-bladed carving knife and starting at the tail end, cut the salmon into paper-thin slices on the diagonal, holding the knife almost horizontally. Carefully detach the slices from the skin. Arrange on a platter and garnish with lemon wedges, dill sprigs, and cold asparagus. Serve with the mustard-dill sauce.

# Warm Vegetable Cake with Camembert and Fruit

YIELD: 6 SERVINGS

1   small zucchini, cut into ¼-inch/6mm dice
2   medium carrots, cut into ¼-inch/6mm dice
5   medium mushrooms, cut into ¼-inch/6mm dice
1¾  cups/320g all-purpose flour
1   teaspoon baking powder
11  tablespoons/165g unsalted butter,
    at room temperature
5   large eggs
    Zest of 1 orange, blanched and
    finely chopped
    Zest of 1 lemon, blanched and
    finely chopped

    Salt and freshly ground black pepper to taste
    Cayenne pepper to taste
3   tablespoons fresh herbs (cilantro,
    marjoram, parsley, or rosemary)
12  ounces/345g Camembert cheese, sliced into
    12 wedges
1   small bunch green grapes
1   small bunch red grapes
3   tablespoons raisins, marinated for 20
    minutes in 1 tablespoon cognac
4   sprigs chervil

1. Preheat the oven to 375°F/190°C. Butter a 9-inch/23cm springform pan and line the bottom with a round of parchment paper. Dust the pan with flour, tilting it to coat evenly and tapping out the excess.

2. Bring a medium saucepan of salted water to a boil. Prepare a medium bowl of ice water. Add the zucchini to the boiling water and boil until partially cooked, about 2 minutes. Remove the zucchini with a strainer and plunge it into the ice water to stop the cooking. Remove the zucchini from the ice water, blot it dry with paper towels, and place in a medium bowl.

3. Repeat the procedure with the carrots (cook for about 3 minutes) and mushrooms (cook for about 1 minute), boiling each separately until partially cooked, shocking them in the ice water, and blotting them dry. Add the carrots and mushrooms to the bowl with the zucchini. Set aside.

4. In another medium bowl, combine the flour and baking powder.

5. In a large bowl, combine the butter, eggs, and zests. Season with salt, pepper, and cayenne. Add half of the flour mixture and stir until combined.

6. Add the reserved vegetables to the remaining flour mixture and stir until combined. Using a rubber spatula, gently fold the vegetable mixture and herbs into the egg mixture until just combined.

7. Pour the batter into the prepared pan and bake for 40 minutes, or until golden brown on top. Remove from the oven, run a sharp knife around the edge of the pan, and remove the ring.

8. To serve, slice the vegetable cake into wedges that are the same size as the Camembert slices. Arrange the vegetable cake wedges, cheese, and grapes decoratively, sprinkling the raisins over the top. Garnish with chervil and serve.

# Salmon Tartare
# with Yogurt-Herb Sauce

YIELD: 2 SERVINGS

## Yogurt-Herb Sauce

2  *tablespoons sour cream*
2  *tablespoons plain yogurt*
1  *tablespoon fresh lemon juice*
1  *tablespoon chopped mixed fresh herbs*
    *(such as parsley, thyme, dill, and chervil)*
    *Salt and freshly ground black pepper to taste*

In a small bowl, combine the sour cream, yogurt, the lemon juice, and herbs. Season with salt and pepper. Cover and refrigerate until needed.

## thyme

Dioscorides, the first-century Greek physician, wrote of thyme's propensity to stimulate amorous instincts, as did Apicius, the first-century Roman cookbook author. The ancient Egyptians agreed, and Europeans still trust thyme in matters of the heart. Like rosemary, a sprig of thyme is used to embellish too many plate presentations these days, simply because it can stand up to the heat and jostling of a restaurant kitchen. Like rosemary, thyme is a brazen herb, and its scent alone can overpower delicate flavors. But that assertiveness pays off sometime after dessert, when you two are getting to know each other better.

## Salmon Tartare

½  *pound/225g salmon meat from the tail,*
    *cut into small pieces*
2  *tablespoons olive oil*
1  *tablespoon fresh lemon juice*
1½  *tablespoons chopped mixed fresh herbs*
    *(such as parsley, thyme, and chervil)*
1  *tablespoon finely chopped shallot*
    *Salt and freshly ground black pepper to taste*
½  *avocado, peeled, pitted, and sliced*
    *Red peppercorns for garnish*

1. On a cutting board, combine the salmon, olive oil, lemon juice, herbs, and shallot. Season with salt and pepper. With a large knife, chop the salmon with the herbs and shallot until very finely mixed. Transfer to a bowl and stir to combine.

2. Form the salmon mixture into heart-shaped patties on 2 plates (you may use a heart-shaped cookie cutter).

3. To serve, arrange an avocado fan on the 2 plates. Spoon some yogurt-herb sauce attractively on the side. Sprinkle with red peppercorns and serve immediately.

# Tuna Tartare with Pink Radish and Curry Mayonnaise

YIELD: 10 CANAPÉS

### Tuna Tartare

4  ounces/120g sushi-quality tuna
1  tablespoon finely chopped radish
1  tablespoon finely chopped celery
1  teaspoon finely minced fresh chives
   Salt and freshly ground black pepper to taste

With a sharp knife, dice the tuna into ¼-inch/6mm cubes. Place in a small bowl. Add the radish, celery, and chives. Toss to combine. Season with salt and pepper. Cover and chill in the refrigerator until needed.

### Curry Mayonnaise

2  teaspoons curry powder
1  teaspoon mango chutney
½  teaspoon ground saffron, preferably Spanish
¼  cup/60ml hot water
1½  teaspoons crème fraîche (page 16)
2  teaspoons prepared mayonnaise
   Salt and freshly ground black pepper to taste

In a small bowl, combine the curry powder, chutney, saffron and hot water. When mixture has cooled, whisk in the créme fraîche and mayonnaise. Season with salt and pepper. Cover and chill in the refrigerator until needed.

### To Assemble

10  baguette slices, lightly brushed with
    olive oil and toasted
10  small arugula leaves
10  thin radish slices
    Ten 2-inch/5cm pieces of fresh chives
10  small celery leaves

1. Add just enough curry dressing to the tuna tartare so that the mixture holds together without being too wet.

2. Top each baguette slice with 1 small arugula leaf. For each canapé, shape a teaspoon of the tartare into a small football-shaped mound using 2 spoons. Place the tartare on the baguette slices. Lean a radish slice against each tartare mound and insert a chive stick and celery leaf in the top. Serve immediately.

## radishes

These root vegetables, bold on the exterior and shy in the middle, cast a spell on lovers centuries ago. As early as 500 B.C., the Egyptians extolled the radish as a coital aid, and the ancient Greeks and Romans agreed. Claude Bigothier published his Latin text, *Raporum Encomium*, or *Eulogy of Radishes*, in 1540 at Lyons. Europeans realized they had much to gain from the wholesome radish—and sometimes more than they bargained for. The Germans categorized radishes with their most potent aphrodisiacs: beans, peas, and lentils. These rosebuds are at their virile best when served clean and cold. Crisp them in ice water if you are in a hurry. Don't bother cutting radishes into frou-frou shapes. After one bite—and one kiss—your aptitude with a paring knife will be the last thing on your lover's mind.

# soups

*Soup is a cure for all our aches and pains—nothing makes us feel better when we*

*stuck with a cold than a bowl of hot chicken soup. Little did you know that soup could be this distinctive or do more than cure the common cold!*

# Marseilles Bouillabaisse

### Rouille

6 cloves garlic
1 small red hot chile pepper, seeded
1 ½ teaspoons kosher salt
1 large egg

1 cup/250ml pure olive oil
1 tablespoon extra-virgin olive oil
Juice of 1 lemon

1. In a food processor, chop the garlic cloves and chile pepper. Add the salt to moisten the puree. Turn off the machine and scrape down the sides.

2. With the motor running, add the egg, then very, very slowly add the pure olive oil, stopping once or twice to scrape down the sides. The mixture should become very thick, like mayonnaise. Season with the extra-virgin olive oil and lemon juice. Transfer to a small nonreactive bowl; cover and chill in the refrigerator until ready to use.

### Soup

4 tablespoons olive oil
1 clove garlic, minced
½ onion, diced
½ carrot, diced
1 stalk celery, diced
½ bulb fennel, diced
3 tablespoons tomato paste
¾ cup/200ml dry white wine
1 ½ cups/375ml fish stock
4 small clams, scrubbed well under cold water

4 mussels, scrubbed well under cold water
6 cherry tomatoes, halved
4 sprigs dill
4 sprigs parsley
2 ounces/60g monkfish, cut into 2-inch cubes
2 ounces/60g sea scallops
2 ounces/60g swordfish, skinned and cut into 2-inch cubes
2 ounces/60g salmon, skinned and cut into 2-inch cubes
2 tablespoons Pernod
8 baguette slices, lightly brushed with olive oil and toasted

1. In a large saucepan, heat 2 tablespoons olive oil over medium-high heat. Add the garlic, onion, carrot, celery, and fennel. Cook, stirring constantly, for 4 minutes.

2. Add the tomato paste to the vegetables and cook, stirring, for another minute. Add the wine and cook until reduced by half, 4 minutes. Add the stock and cook until reduced by half, 6 minutes. Add the clams, mussels, tomatoes, dill, and parsley. Cook until the clams and mussels open. Discard any mussels or clams that do not open.

3. Heat the remaining 2 tablespoons oil in a large skillet over medium heat. Add the monkfish, scallops, swordfish, and salmon and sear until golden on the outside but still rare inside. Add the Pernod and scrape up any browned bits from the bottom of the skillet. Add the contents of the skillet to the simmering soup and cook gently for 2 minutes more.

4. To serve, divide the soup among 4 warmed soup bowls. Accompany with the baguette slices spread with the rouille.

# Mussel and Leek Soup

YIELD: 6 SERVINGS

½ cup/10g fresh basil leaves
3 cloves garlic, 2 smashed, 1 whole
¼ cup/60ml olive oil
    Salt and freshly ground black pepper to taste
6 baguette slices
2 ½ pounds/1kg mussels, scrubbed well under cold water
1 cup/140g chopped onion
½ cup/70g chopped celery
½ cup/70g chopped parsnips
1 tablespoon chopped fresh thyme
1 ½ cups/375ml dry white wine

4 Roma tomatoes
5 tablespoons/75g unsalted butter
¾ cup/100g finely diced fennel
¾ cup/100g finely diced carrot
3 cups/420g chopped leeks
6 cups/1.5l fish, seafood, or chicken stock
8 threads saffron
3 large egg yolks
1 ½ cups/375ml heavy cream
    Cayenne pepper to taste
    Old Bay Seasoning to taste

1. In a blender, combine the basil, smashed garlic, and oil. Blend until smooth. Season with salt and pepper. Spread the baguette slices with the basil mixture and reserve to garnish the soup.

2. Remove the beards from the mussels and discard any that are open. In a stockpot with a lid, combine the mussels, onion, celery, parsnips, whole garlic, ½ tablespoon thyme, and the wine over medium heat. Cover and steam for 2 minutes, shaking the pot occasionally. Begin checking the mussels; as they open, transfer them to a colander placed over a bowl. Total steaming time will be about 4 minutes. Discard any mussels that do not open.

3. Strain the mussel broth—in the cooking pot and in the bowl—through a fine sieve lined with cheesecloth into a small bowl. Set aside. Remove the shells from the mussels. Set the mussels aside.

4. In a medium saucepan, bring 2 quarts/2 liters water to a boil. Meanwhile, with a paring knife, cut out the stems from the tomatoes and make a small "X" in the opposite ends. Working in batches, plunge the tomatoes in the boiling water and leave them in just until the skins are loosened, 10 to 20 seconds. With a slotted spoon, remove the tomatoes and place them in a large bowl of cold water until cool enough to handle. Slip off the skins and cut the tomatoes in half. Gently but firmly squeeze the seeds from the halves. Finely dice the tomatoes and set aside.

5. In a large saucepan, melt the butter over medium heat. Add the fennel, carrot, and leeks. Cook, stirring, until the vegetables are softened, about 5 minutes. Add the reserved mussel broth, stock, and saffron. Bring to a boil; reduce the heat to medium-low and simmer for 15 minutes.

6. In a medium bowl, whisk the egg yolks and the heavy cream until well combined. Whisking constantly, slowly add 1 cup/250ml of the simmering stock. When the cup of stock is fully incorporated, add the egg yolk mixture to the simmering stock and immediately reduce the heat to low. Do not let the soup return to a boil.

7. Preheat the oven to 350°F/180°C. Add the reserved mussels, reserved tomatoes, and remaining ½ tablespoon thyme to the soup. Season with salt, cayenne pepper, and Old Bay Seasoning.

8. To serve, place the reserved basil croutons in the oven and toast until golden on the edges. Divide the soup among 6 warmed soup bowls and serve with the baguette slices.

## carrots

One of mankind's oldest foodstuffs and most enduring aphrodisiacs, carrots have been cultivated for thousands of years. The Greeks used carrots to cure sexual ills, and the Arabs served them with milk sauce as a coital aid. Recent research indicates that the ancients were not far off base. Carrots are a prime source of vitamin A, a necessary nutrient in the production of all sex hormones in both men and women. In men, vitamin A contributes to a healthy prostate and testes and increases the number of sperm in each ejaculation. Furthermore, carrots supply an estrogen-like compound that stimulates the sexual appetite in both sexes. Rumors concerning carrots' invaluable role in preserving your eyesight are all true—and you'll need those eyes to watch your partner linger over the last bite.

# Oyster Soup with Spinach

18 oysters, scrubbed well under cold water
18 large spinach leaves, well washed
¾ cup/200ml dry white wine
5 cups/1.2l fish, seafood, or chicken stock
3 tablespoons Pernod

3 large egg yolks
1 ½ cups/375ml heavy cream
Salt and cayenne pepper to taste
¼ cup/5g fresh basil leaves, cut into julienne strips

1. With an oyster knife, carefully open the oysters, pouring the liquor into a cup as you shuck. Add the beards to the cup with the juices and set aside. Set aside the oysters separately.

2. Bring a small saucepan of water to a boil. Prepare a small bowl of ice water. Add the spinach leaves to the pan and blanch for a few seconds. Remove with a sieve and place in the bowl of ice water. Drain well. Wrap each oyster in a spinach leaf.

3. In a large wide saucepan, bring the wine to a simmer over medium heat. Gently add the spinach-wrapped oysters and poach until the oysters are firm, approximately 1 minute. With a slotted spoon, transfer the oysters in their wrapping to a platter and set aside.

4. Add the stock, reserved oyster liquor and beards, and Pernod to the poaching liquid. Simmer gently for 5 minutes. Strain through a fine sieve lined with cheesecloth into a medium saucepan. Return to a simmer over medium heat.

5. In a medium bowl, whisk the egg yolks and cream until well combined. Whisking constantly, slowly add 1 cup/250ml of the simmering stock. When the cup of stock is fully incorporated, add the egg yolk mixture to the simmering stock and immediately reduce the heat to low. Do not let the soup return to a boil. Season with salt and cayenne pepper.

6. To serve, divide the reserved oysters among 6 soup bowls. Ladle the soup over the oysters, sprinkle with the basil and serve immediately.

## spinach

Now that you're not a kid anymore, make the first move and bring home a bundle of fresh spinach. Popeye didn't win Olive Oyl's heart on the basis of his sparkling personality; suffice it to say, she knew of this superfood's ribald reputation. Steaming it brings out its lush color and flavor while preserving its supply of iron, potassium, and vitamins. Those will come in handy later, after you've cleared the table. (And speaking of seduction, when was the last time you put that table to good use?)

# Pea Soup

*2 ½ pounds/1kg fresh unshelled peas, rinsed thoroughly*
*4 cups/1l vegetable stock*
*6 tablespoons/90g unsalted butter*
*6 shallots, finely chopped*

*Salt and freshly ground white pepper to taste*
*3 sprigs mint*
*8 stalks chives, chopped*

1. Shell the peas, reserving the pods, and set aside. In a large saucepan, combine the stock and pea pods over medium heat. Bring to a simmer and cook, stirring occasionally, for ½ hour, or until the stock takes on a pronounced fresh pea flavor. Strain the stock into a bowl and chill, covered, in the refrigerator or freezer until cold.

2. In a soup pot, melt the butter over medium-high heat. Add the shallots and reduce the heat to medium. Cook, stirring, until the shallots are softened but not colored, 3 to 4 minutes. Add the peas and just enough of the vegetable stock to cover (rechill the remaining stock). Season with salt and white pepper. Bring the stock to a simmer and cook the peas until they are tender but still retain a bright green color. Remove from the heat and strain (save the cooking liquid for another use).

3. Transfer the peas to a blender or food processor and puree on medium speed, in batches if necessary, using the chilled vegetable stock as needed to achieve a smooth, light consistency. (Using chilled stock will stop the peas from cooking further, so their bright color and flavor are maintained.) Add the mint and puree until smooth.

4. Strain the soup through a medium sieve into a saucepan to remove the skins. Adjust the seasoning with salt and pepper. Serve hot or cold, garnished with the chives.

## peas

The French call them *petits pois*, but their consequences are far from small. Green peas lend men and women the verve to instigate and the stamina to enjoy. I imagine that countless ancient and modern people have followed Nefzawí's stimulating recipe from *The Perfumed Garden*: green peas boiled with onions, then powdered with cinnamon, ginger, and cardamom. Indeed, such a combination of potent aphrodisiacs was not intended for the faint of heart. Today's boiled peas are simply adorned with a bit of parsley, onion, and butter; they bring the playfulness of springtime to your table for two all year round.

# Potato-Corn Soup with Cilantro Pesto

YIELD: 4 SERVINGS

## Cilantro Pesto

YIELD: 1 CUP/250ML

*2 ounces/60g fresh cilantro*
*3 cloves garlic*
*2 ounces/60g pine nuts*
*2 ounces/60g grated Parmesan cheese*
  *About ¼ cup/60ml olive oil*

Place everything except the oil in a food processor or blender. Puree on medium speed, adding enough olive oil to reach the desired consistency. If you are making this in advance and freezing or storing in the refrigerator, add the cheese right before using.

## Soup

*½ teaspoon olive oil*
*½ cup/70g chopped onion*
*½ stalk celery, chopped*
*½ medium carrot, chopped*
*½ medium potato, peeled and chopped*
*1 medium red bell pepper, cored, seeded, and chopped*
*½ cup/75g chopped green bell pepper*
*1 small clove garlic, chopped*
*½ jalapeño pepper*

*1 tablespoon chopped fresh oregano*
*1 small zucchini, sliced into rounds*
*1 small yellow squash, sliced into rounds*
*2 cups/500ml vegetable stock made with onions, leeks, turnips, squash, tomato, and garlic*
*3 ½ cups/670g fresh corn kernels*
  *Salt and freshly ground black pepper to taste*
*3 teaspoons cilantro pesto (recipe above)*

1. In a soup pot, heat the oil over medium heat. Add the onion, celery, carrot, and potato. Sauté until the onion is golden, 5 to 6 minutes. Add the bell peppers, garlic, jalapeño, oregano, zucchini, and yellow squash and sauté for 2 minutes. Add the stock and simmer for 5 minutes.

2. Strain the soup through a medium sieve into a clean soup pot, reserving the solids. Add half the vegetable solids to the pot (you can remove the jalapeño if you wish) and place the remaining solids in the bowl of a food processor. Pulse the vegetables until a chunky puree forms, 10 seconds. Stir the puree into the soup and add the corn. Simmer for 10 minutes more. Season with salt and pepper and serve immediately with cilantro pesto, either on top or on the side.

# onions

The onion's form and sulfuric pungency have attracted humans since the beginning of time; it is believed that prehistoric clans cultivated them in the Fertile Crescent long before the era of agriculture. Later civilizations, including the Egyptians, Greeks, and Arabs, left extensive advice regarding this member of the lily family as a coital aid. The Romans were especially fond of the onion. The poet Ovid (43 B.C.–A.D. 17) recommended the onion in his poem on the art of love, "Ars Amatoria." Apicius, the first-century Roman cookbook author, suggested onion cooked in water with pine seeds or cress juice and pepper. Martial, the poet and epigrammatist (A.D. 40–104), advised, "If your wife is old and your member is exhausted, eat onions in plenty." Plan on a good cry when chopping strong yellow and white onions. Consider it an exercise in expressing your deeper emotions. Save your mild sweeties, such as Vidalias, Walla Wallas, and Italian reds, for salads and sandwiches. Better yet, mince and serve with caviar on toast. In bed. Notice your lover wiping away a tear? Those are tears of joy, my friend.

# Four-Onion Soup

Y I E L D :  4  S E R V I N G S

2 tablespoons/30g unsalted butter or vegetable oil
3 medium white onions, thinly sliced
3 red onions, thinly sliced
12 shallots, thinly sliced
4 leeks, washed and thinly sliced
2 cups/500ml dry red wine
3 cups/750ml beef stock
1 bay leaf
2 teaspoons freshly ground black pepper

Salt to taste
4 slices French baguette
2 large egg yolks
2 tablespoons heavy cream
½ cup/125ml dry sherry
4 thin slices Swiss cheese
4 thin slices provolone cheese
2 tablespoons grated Parmesan cheese

1. In a large wide saucepan, heat the butter or oil over medium heat. Add the onions, shallots, and leeks. Cook, stirring frequently, until golden and caramelized, about 12 minutes. Add the wine and bring to a simmer. Reduce the liquid for 7 to 9 minutes. Add the stock, bay leaf, and pepper. Season with salt. Return to a simmer and cook for 45 minutes.

2. Meanwhile, preheat the broiler. Lightly butter the French baguette and toast it until golden. Set aside.

3. In a medium bowl, whisk the egg yolks and heavy cream. Whisking constantly, slowly add 1 cup/250ml simmering soup. When the cup is fully incorporated, add the egg yolk mixture to the simmering soup and immediately reduce the heat to low. Stir in the sherry. Do not let the soup return to a boil.

4. To serve, divide the soup among 4 heatproof soup bowls. Top each soup with a piece of toast, a slice of Swiss cheese, and a slice of provolone. Sprinkle Parmesan over the top. Place the soup bowls under the broiler and heat until the cheese turns golden brown. Serve immediately.

# Roasted Garlic Soup Provençal

Yield: 8 servings

5 whole heads garlic
2 tablespoons olive oil
   Salt and freshly ground black pepper to taste
4 ripe beefsteak tomatoes
1 teaspoon sherry vinegar
1 tablespoon olive oil
½ red onion, finely chopped
2 tablespoons chopped fresh parsley
3 leaves fresh basil, chopped

1 teaspoon chopped fresh thyme
2 tablespoons/30g unsalted butter
10 shallots, finely chopped
6 cups/1.5l chicken stock
1 tablespoon chopped fresh thyme
1 bay leaf
8 large egg yolks
¾ cup/200ml heavy cream
½ cup/125ml dry sherry

1. To roast the garlic, preheat the oven to 325°F/160°C. Pull the papery husks off the garlic heads. Slice the tip off each head to expose the cloves. Rub with the olive oil and season with salt and pepper. Place in an ovenproof dish, sprinkle with a bit of water and cover with aluminum foil. Roast for 30 to 45 minutes, or until very tender. Let cool. Squeeze the garlic pulp from the skins into a bowl, setting aside 3 cloves of pulp for the tomato provençal.

2. In a medium saucepan, bring 2 quarts/2 liters water to a boil. Meanwhile, with a paring knife, cut out the stems from the tomatoes and make a small "X" in the opposite ends. Plunge the tomatoes in the boiling water and leave them in just until the skins are loosened, 10 to 20 seconds. With a slotted spoon, remove the tomatoes and rinse them under cold water until cool enough to handle. Slip off the skins and cut the tomatoes in half. Gently but firmly squeeze the seeds from the tomato halves. Cut into medium dice. Set aside.

3. In a medium bowl, whisk the vinegar and oil. Just before serving, prepare the tomato provençal by adding 3 cloves of the roasted garlic to the diced tomato, onion, parsley, basil, and thyme.

4. Meanwhile, in a large, heavy skillet, melt the butter over medium heat. Add the shallots and cook, stirring, until soft and transparent, 10 to 12 minutes. (Do not let them brown.) Stir in the remaining garlic pulp, stock, thyme, and bay leaf. Season with salt and pepper. Bring to a boil, reduce the heat to low, and simmer for 45 minutes. Remove from the heat and let cool for 10 minutes. Remove the bay leaf.

5. Working in 3 batches, puree the soup in the bowl of a food processor. Puree each batch and strain through a fine sieve lined with cheesecloth into a medium saucepan. Bring the soup to a simmer over medium heat.

6. In a medium bowl, whisk the egg yolks, heavy cream, and sherry until well combined. Whisking constantly, slowly add 1 cup/250ml simmering soup. When the cup of soup is fully incorporated, add the egg yolk mixture to the simmering soup and immediately reduce the heat to low. Do not let the soup return to a boil.

7. To serve, divide the soup among 8 warmed soup bowls. Spoon a dollop of tomato provençal in the center of each bowl and serve immediately with crusty bread.

# garlic

The "stinking rose" is actually a member of the lily family, and its notorious odor makes it one arduous food that Aphrodite would advise you *both* to consume at the same sitting. For centuries the world has recognized garlic as more than just another sex-enhancing bulb. The ancient Greeks and Romans knew of its medicinal powers, and the ancient Egyptians of the fourteenth century B.C. were sure to send King Tutankhamen into the afterlife well stocked. Garlic fans have long reveled in the sexual signals it sends; at one time Palestinian grooms sometimes wore a clove in their buttonhole to ensure a successful wedding night.

Apart from deterring serpents and scorpions of lore, garlic also thwarts viruses, bacteria, and fungi in the laboratory. Therefore scientists today are exploring the plausibility of common wisdom, for garlic has been used to treat dozens of ailments, including arthritis, infections, measles, and typhoid. Hopefully, their findings will not spur us to rely on garlic solely for its curative powers, for its pungent flavor puts a spring in the step that others always find attractive. Indulge together. You will both feel garlic's heady glow and relish each other's passionate exhalations.

# Vegetable Soup
# with Fennel

YIELD: 6 SERVINGS

2 ripe large tomatoes
2 cups/400g great Northern beans, picked over for
    stones, covered in 2 inches water, and soaked overnight
2 fresh pork hocks or 1 fresh and 1 smoked pork hock
2 large russet potatoes, preferably Idaho, peeled
2 large carrots, peeled
5 fresh bay leaves
¼ cup/60ml olive oil

4 cloves garlic, finely chopped
1 pound/454g spinach, shredded
1 pound/454g Swiss chard, shredded
1 pound/454g fennel bulbs, finely diced
½ cup/95g fresh corn kernels
½ cup/95g fresh shelled peas
    Salt and freshly ground black pepper to taste

## fennel

Some say salmon with fennel is a match made in heaven; also try the fragrant leaves and seeds with mackerel, in salads, and as an accompaniment to lamb. Fennel also turns up in Vatsayana's discourse on the "means of increasing sexual vigor." Fennel juice and milk are combined with ghee (clarified butter), honey, sugar, and licorice to create a holy nectar "provocative of sexual vigor." Those in the Mediterranean region also vouch for fennel's amatory effect and have been know to serve fennel soup to stir up some excitement. Nibble on a few seeds after dessert, as the Indians do, to sweeten the breath and provoke carnality.

1. In a stockpot, bring 5 quarts/5 liters water to a boil. Meanwhile, with a paring knife, cut out the stems from the tomatoes and make a small "X" in the opposite ends. Plunge the tomatoes in the boiling water and leave them in just until the skins are loosened, 10 to 20 seconds. With a slotted spoon, remove the tomatoes and rinse them under cold water until cool enough to handle. Set aside.

2. Add the drained beans, pork hocks, potatoes, carrots, and bay leaves to the boiling water. Return to a boil.

3. Meanwhile, slip the skins off the tomatoes and cut the tomatoes in half. Gently but firmly squeeze the seeds from the tomato halves. Chop coarsely. In a skillet, heat the oil over medium heat. Add the garlic and cook, stirring, until golden. Add the chopped tomatoes and cook for 10 minutes more. Transfer the contents of the skillet to the boiling pot. Reduce the heat and simmer gently, covered, for 1 hour.

4. Meanwhile, in a large saucepan, bring 3 quarts/3 liters water to a boil. Add the spinach, Swiss chard, fennel, corn, and peas. Return the water to a boil, reduce the heat, and simmer for 10 minutes. Drain the vegetables and set aside.

5. When the pot of beans has simmered for 1 hour, remove the carrots and the potatoes and transfer them to a bowl. Mash them together with a fork or potato masher and return them to the pot. Add the reserved parboiled vegetables and season with salt and pepper. Continue simmering, uncovered, for 30 minutes, skimming and stirring as necessary.

6. To serve, remove the pork hocks and the bay leaves. (The meat from the hocks may be eaten separately or diced into the soup.) Adjust the seasoning with salt and pepper and serve immediately with crusty Italian bread or focaccia.

# Spicy Crab and Clam Chowder

YIELD: 6 SERVINGS

2 tablespoons extra-virgin olive oil

2 tablespoons minced garlic

2 tablespoons minced shallots

1 small onion, cut into ¼-inch/6mm dice

1 medium carrot, cut into ¼-inch/6mm dice

1 stalk celery, cut into ¼-inch/6mm dice

1 jalapeño pepper, seeded and
   finely chopped

1 cup/200g diced Roma tomato

1 tablespoon tomato paste

Salt and cayenne pepper to taste

2 quarts/2l fish stock

1 cup/250ml fresh or canned clam juice

1 cup/250ml heavy cream

1 quart/900g clams, shucked

½ pound/225g fresh lump crabmeat,
   picked over for shells

1 ear fresh corn, kernels removed

1 bay leaf

1 large russet potato, cut into ¼-inch/6mm dice

1. In a stockpot, heat the oil over medium heat. Add the garlic, shallots, onion, carrot, and celery. Cook, stirring, until tender, about 20 minutes. Add the jalapeño, tomato, and tomato paste. Cook, stirring, for 2 minutes. Season with salt and cayenne pepper.

2. Add the remaining ingredients and bring to a boil. Reduce the heat and simmer, stirring occasionally, for 30 minutes. Remove the bay leaf. Divide among soup bowls and serve immediately.

# Cold Avocado Soup
# with Crabmeat

YIELD: 2 SERVINGS

*2 large avocados, peeled, pitted, and cut into chunks*
*1 cup/250ml chicken stock, chilled*
*¼ cup/60ml dry white wine*
*½ teaspoon mild curry powder*
*½ teaspoon salt*

*Freshly ground black pepper to taste*
*1 cup/250ml half-and-half*
*¼ pound/120g lump fresh or frozen crabmeat*
*2 teaspoons salmon roe*

1. In a blender, combine the avocado, stock, wine, curry powder, salt, and pepper. Puree until smooth. Add the half-and-half and blend until incorporated.

2. To serve, divide the soup between 2 chilled soup bowls. Top each bowl with a large piece of crabmeat and a teaspoon of salmon roe. Serve immediately.

---

# Chilled Oyster Soup

YIELD: 2 SERVINGS

*1 tablespoon/15g unsalted butter*
*1 large leek, white and light green parts only, thinly sliced*
*1 cup/250ml consommé*
*6 large oysters, such as Malpeque, scrubbed well*
*1 stalk lemon grass, outer leaves discarded, coarsely chopped*

*1 leaf gelatin, softened in 2 tablespoons warm water*
*½ cup/125ml heavy cream*
*Salt and freshly ground black pepper to taste*
*2 ounces/60g caviar (any kind)*
*½ lime, cut into 4 wedges*

1. In a medium skillet, melt the butter over medium heat. Add the leek and cook, stirring, until softened, approximately 2 minutes. Set aside.

2. In a large saucepan, bring the consommé to a boil. Add the oysters. Cover and steam for 2 minutes, shaking the pot occasionally. As the oysters open, transfer to a plate. Discard the shells and any oysters that do not open. Wrap in plastic and refrigerate.

3. Strain the consommé through a fine sieve lined with cheesecloth into a small saucepan. Add the lemon grass and bring to a boil over high heat. Reduce the heat to low and simmer until the lemon grass has infused the consommé, about 10 minutes.

4. Add the gelatin and cream to the consommé and continue to simmer, stirring, until the gelatin is dissolved, about 1 minute. Remove from the heat and strain through a medium sieve into a medium bowl. Place the bowl in a larger bowl of ice water to chill the sauce quickly until it is a thick, syrupy consistency. Season with salt and pepper.

5. To serve, spoon the leeks on the bottom half of 2 soup plates. Place 3 oysters on the top half of each plate. Ladle the soup lightly over the leeks and oysters and top each oyster with some caviar. Garnish with a lime wedge and serve.

# Andalusian Gazpacho

YIELD: 5 OR 6 SERVINGS

### Gazpacho

*1 pound/454g ripe tomatoes*

*2 cucumbers, peeled, seeded, and coarsely chopped*

*1 stalk celery, coarsely chopped*

*1 bunch scallions, white part only, coarsely chopped*

*1 red bell pepper, cored, seeded, and coarsely chopped*

*1 small clove garlic, boiled in water for 3 minutes and drained*

*½ cup/125ml chicken or vegetable stock*

*2 fresh basil leaves*

*2 tablespoons red wine vinegar*

*3 drops Tabasco sauce*

*1 tablespoon olive oil*

*½ teaspoon sugar (optional)*

*Salt and freshly ground black pepper to taste*

1. In a large saucepan, bring 2 quarts/2 liters water to a boil. Meanwhile, with a paring knife, cut out the stems from the tomatoes and make a small "X" in the opposite ends. Working in batches, plunge the tomatoes in the boiling water and leave them in just until the skins are loosened, 10 to 20 seconds. With a slotted spoon, remove the tomatoes and place them in a large bowl of cold water until cool enough to handle. Slip off the skins and cut the tomatoes in half. Gently but firmly squeeze the seeds from the halves. Chop coarsely.

2. In a blender, combine the tomatoes, cucumber, celery, scallions, bell pepper, and garlic. Add the stock and puree until smooth. (For an extra-smooth consistency, put through a food mill or strainer to remove any bits of skin or seeds.)

3. Add the basil, vinegar, Tabasco, oil, and sugar if using. Blend until thoroughly mixed. Season with salt and pepper. Cover and refrigerate until ice cold.

### Garnishes

*1 slice white bread, trimmed of crust*

*½ cup/125ml olive oil*

*1 small clove garlic*

*1 Roma tomato, peeled (see above), seeded, and finely diced*

*½ small cucumber, peeled, seeded, and finely diced*

*½ large green bell pepper, cored, seeded, and finely diced*

*Parsley sprigs*

1. Cut the bread into ¼-inch/6mm dice. In a small skillet, heat the oil over medium heat. Add the garlic and cook until browned. Remove and discard the garlic.

2. Add the diced bread to the hot oil and sauté quickly until nicely browned. Remove the croutons with a slotted spoon and drain on paper towels.

3. To serve, ladle the gazpacho into chilled bowls and surround with crushed ice. Sprinkle with the tomato, cucumber, bell pepper, and croutons and garnish with parsley.

# Roasted White Peach Soup

YIELD: 4 SERVINGS

4 ripe large white peaches, peeled, halved, and pitted
1 ½ cups/345g sugar
2 cups/500ml peach juice, plus extra if needed
1 vanilla bean, split and seeds extracted
1 star anise, cracked

Juice of 3 oranges
Juice of 2 lemons
½ pint/150g strawberries, washed
2 sprigs mint

1. Preheat the oven to 400°F/200°C. Lightly coat a baking sheet with butter. Place the peach halves, cut side down, on the prepared baking sheet. Sprinkle the peaches with ½ cup sugar and bake for 15 to 20 minutes, until well roasted.

2. Transfer the peaches to a food processor, along with any drippings from the baking sheet. Puree until smooth, stopping 2 or 3 times to scrape down the sides. Transfer to a large bowl and set aside.

3. In a small saucepan, combine the peach juice, remaining 1 cup sugar, vanilla bean, and star anise over medium heat. Bring to a boil and then remove from the heat. Let the syrup infuse for about 1 hour in a warm place. Strain through a fine sieve and add the citrus juices.

4. Tasting as you go, slowly add the peach syrup to the peach puree until the desired flavor is achieved. If the soup is nicely flavored but too thick, thin it with a little plain peach juice. Cover and chill in the refrigerator until completely cold.

5. To serve, ladle the soup into chilled soup plates or cups and garnish with the strawberries and mint sprigs.

## anise

This plant native to the eastern Mediterranean provides oil and lusty little seeds that taste much like licorice. The ancient Romans added the seeds to their wedding cakes, and anise still finds its way into Italian pastries and liqueurs today. To release their full flavor, crush the seeds with a rolling pin or a mortar and pestle. Close your eyes and breathe in the sensual aroma.

# Chilled Cucumber and Dill Soup

YIELD: 4 TO 6 SERVINGS

4 tablespoons/60g unsalted butter
2 medium cucumbers, peeled and thinly sliced
2 cups/500ml dry white wine
2 medium shallots, finely chopped
4 white mushrooms, diced

2 quarts/2l fish stock
2 cups/500ml heavy cream
2 tablespoons chopped fresh dill, plus 6 sprigs
for garnish

1. In a large saucepan, melt the butter over medium heat. Add all but 6 slices cucumber and cook, stirring, until very tender, about 20 minutes. Remove from the heat. Set aside.

2. In a medium nonreactive saucepan, combine the wine, shallots, and mushrooms. Bring to a simmer and cook, stirring, until reduced by 90 percent. Add the stock and simmer, stirring, for 15 minutes. Add the cream and simmer for 10 minutes more. Remove from the heat.

3. In a blender, combine the sautéed cucumbers, cream mixture, and chopped dill. Blend until smooth. Strain through a fine sieve into a bowl. Cover and chill in the refrigerator. Serve the soup garnished with the reserved cucumber slices and the dill sprigs.

# Tomato Soup
# with Basil Guacamole

## Soup

5  ripe tomatoes
1  cup/250ml olive oil
2  onions, thickly sliced
2  leeks, white part only, washed and thickly sliced
1  bulb fennel, thickly sliced
2  stalks celery, thickly sliced
2  large red bell peppers, cored, seeded, and coarsely chopped

4  large cloves garlic
2  tablespoons tomato paste
4  cups/1l chicken stock
1  bouquet garni (1 bay leaf and 2 sprigs each thyme and parsley, bundled in a piece of cheesecloth and tied with string)
   Salt and freshly ground black pepper to taste
3  cups/750ml tomato juice

1. In a large saucepan, bring 2 quarts/2 liters water to a boil. Meanwhile, with a paring knife, cut out the stems from the tomatoes and make a small "X" in the opposite ends. Working in batches, plunge the tomatoes in the boiling water and leave them in just until the skins are loosened, 10 to 20 seconds. With a slotted spoon, remove the tomatoes and place them in a large bowl of cold water until cool enough to handle. Slip off the skins and cut the tomatoes in half. Gently but firmly squeeze the seeds from the halves. Chop the tomatoes coarsely and set aside.

2. In a Dutch oven or soup pot, heat the oil over medium-high heat. Add the onions, leeks, fennel, celery, bell peppers, and garlic. Cook, stirring fre-quently, until the vegetables are softened, 15 to 20 minutes. Add the tomato paste and cook, stirring, for 3 minutes. Add the stock and bouquet garni and bring to a boil. Season with salt and pepper. Reduce heat to medium and simmer, stirring occa-sionally, for 20 minutes.

3. Add the reserved tomatoes. Bring the soup to a boil and then remove it from the heat. Set it aside to cool. When cool, discard the bouquet garni and transfer the soup, in batches, to a blender. Puree until smooth. Add the tomato juice and season with salt and pepper. Strain through a fine sieve into a clean bowl; cover and chill in the refrigerator until ready to serve.

## Basil Guacamole

4   ripe avocados, peeled and pitted
20  fresh basil leaves, 4 left whole, the remainder chopped

Fresh lemon juice to taste
Tabasco or other hot sauce to taste
Salt and freshly ground black pepper to taste

1. In a medium bowl, combine the avocado, chop-ped basil, and lemon juice. With a fork, crush the avocado and mix well, still keeping a chunky con-sistency. Season with Tabasco, salt, and pepper.

2. To serve, ladle the soup into chilled soup bowls. Spoon a large dollop of basil guacamole in the mid-dle and garnish with the whole basil leaves.

## basil

Illustrious Italian cooks spice up nearly every tomato dish with aromatic basil, which is at its best when freshly minced. This pun-gent member of the mint family is considered the "royal herb" of several cultures, and women find it prevents their men from roam-ing too far astray. Some Italians enjoy basil's alluring effect by serving sprigs in tiny vases. And who knows? A bouquet of basil may beat even roses when seducing your mate.

# entrees

*These entrees span the globe in terms of flavor and variety—but all are guaranteed to make your taste buds tingle and scorch the fires of passion.*

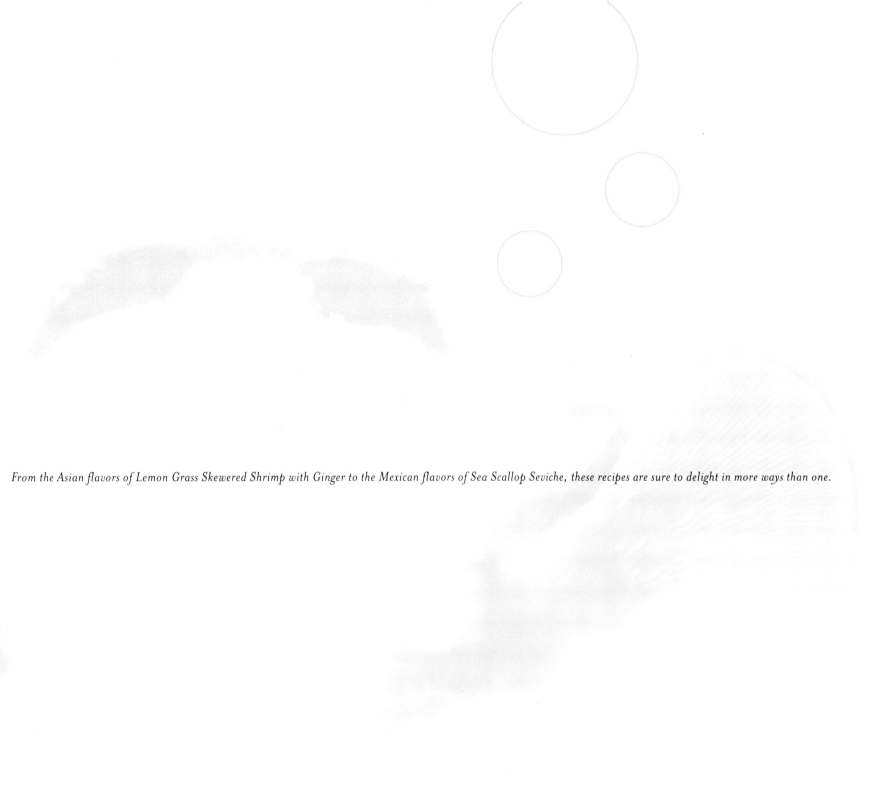

From the Asian flavors of Lemon Grass Skewered Shrimp with Ginger to the Mexican flavors of Sea Scallop Seviche, these recipes are sure to delight in more ways than one.

# Steamed Mussels with Curry, Saffron, and Lemon Grass

YIELD: 2 SERVINGS

1 tablespoon/15g unsalted butter

1 tablespoon finely chopped shallot

2 cloves garlic, finely chopped

2 teaspoons curry powder

½ teaspoon ground saffron

¼ stalk lemon grass, outer leaves discarded, coarsely chopped

½ cup/125ml dry white wine

⅓ cup/75ml heavy cream

1 pound/454g large mussels, such as Penn Cove, debearded and well washed

1 tablespoon thinly sliced scallions

Pinch freshly ground black pepper

1. In a large saucepan, melt the butter over medium heat. Add the shallot and garlic and cook, stirring, until softened, 4 minutes. Add the curry powder, saffron, and lemon grass and cook, stirring, for 8 minutes more. Add the wine and cream and bring to a boil.

2. Add the mussels. Cover and steam for 2 minutes, shaking the pan occasionally. Begin checking the mussels; as they open, transfer them to 2 large soup bowls. Total steaming time will be 4 to 6 minutes. Discard any mussels that do not open.

3. Bring the mussel broth to a boil over high heat. Add the scallions and pepper. Spoon the broth over the mussels and serve immediately with French baguette.

# Tagliatelle with Rock Shrimp, Scallops, and Tomatoes

YIELD: 4 SERVINGS

6 ripe medium tomatoes
3 tablespoons olive oil
1 clove garlic, minced
½ cup/70g diced onion
¼ cup/5g chopped fresh thyme
⅓ cup/60g diced celery
⅓ cup/60g diced carrot

⅓ cup/60g diced leeks, white part only
  Salt and freshly ground black pepper to taste
1 pound/454g dried tagliatelle or fettuccine
½ pound/225g rock shrimp, peeled and deveined
½ pound/225g sea scallops
¼ cup/5g chopped fresh parsley

1. In a stockpot, bring 1 gallon/4 liters water to a boil. Meanwhile, with a paring knife, cut out the stems from the tomatoes and make a small "X" in the opposite ends. Working in batches, plunge the tomatoes in the boiling water and leave them in just until the skins are loosened, 10 to 20 seconds. With a slotted spoon, remove the tomatoes and place them in a large bowl of ice water until cool enough to handle. Slip off the skins and cut the tomatoes in half. Gently but firmly squeeze the seeds from the halves. Chop coarsely.

2. In a medium skillet, heat 1 ½ tablespoons oil over medium-high heat. Add the garlic, onion, and thyme. Cook, stirring, until the onion is softened and translucent. (Do not let the onion brown.) Add the celery, carrot, and leeks. Cook, stirring, until all the vegetables are softened. Add the tomatoes and cook, stirring, for 15 minutes. Season with salt and pepper. Reserve and keep warm.

3. Meanwhile, cook the tagliatelle in a stockpot of boiling salted water until al dente, 6 to 8 minutes. Drain and drizzle with a bit of olive oil to prevent sticking.

4. In a large skillet, heat the remaining 1 ½ tablespoons oil over high heat. Add the shrimp and scallops. Cook, stirring, until the shrimp turn pink, about 2 minutes. Add the reserved vegetables with the sauce and pasta and mix thoroughly. Divide the tagliatelle between 2 plates and sprinkle with parsley. Enjoy the leftovers with your lover the next day.

# Spaghetti with Lobster Bolognese

YIELD: 2 SERVINGS

½ pound/225g dried spaghetti
2 lobster tails, cooked and cooled
3 ripe Roma tomatoes
2 tablespoons olive oil
1 clove garlic, minced
½ onion, minced

½ carrot, minced
½ stalk celery, minced
½ bulb fennel, minced
2 cups/500ml chicken stock
1 tablespoon chopped fresh parsley
Salt and freshly ground black pepper to taste

1. Cook the spaghetti in a large stockpot of boiling salted water until al dente, 6 to 8 minutes. Drain and drizzle with a bit of olive oil to prevent sticking.

2. Remove the lobster meat from the shells, saving the shells for garnish, and place the meat in a meat grinder fitted with a ¼-inch/6mm die. Grind the lobster and set aside.

3. In a large saucepan, bring 2 cups/500ml water to a boil. Meanwhile, with a paring knife, cut out the stems from the tomatoes and make a small "X" in the opposite ends. Working in batches, plunge the tomatoes in the boiling water and leave them in just until the skins are loosened, 10 to 20 seconds. With a slotted spoon, remove the tomatoes and place them in a large bowl of cold water until cool enough to handle. Slip off the skins and cut the tomatoes in half. Gently but firmly squeeze the seeds from the halves. Dice the tomatoes.

4. In a large skillet, heat the oil over medium-high heat. Add the garlic and onion and cook, stirring, until the onion is softened, about 15 minutes. Add the carrot, celery, and fennel. Cook, stirring, until the vegetables are tender, about 15 minutes. Add the tomatoes and cook, stirring, for 5 minutes more.

5. Add the stock and bring to a simmer. Cook, stirring, for 1 minute. Add the ground lobster and cook, stirring, for 2 to 3 minutes, to reduce the stock slightly. Add the parsley and season with salt and pepper.

6. To serve, add the spaghetti to the sauce and toss until all the ingredients are heated through. Garnish with the lobster tail shells. Serve immediately.

# Mediterranean Spaghetti with Seafood

YIELD: 2 SERVINGS

2 tablespoons sea salt
2 Roma tomatoes
1 lemon, cut into 1/8-inch/3mm-thick slices
2 sprigs thyme
4 tablespoons olive oil
2 medium shallots, finely chopped
2 cloves garlic, finely chopped
4 tablespoons dry white wine
1/4 pound/120g mussels, debearded and well washed
6 clams, scrubbed well

2 large shrimp, peeled and deveined
2 large sea scallops
1/2 pound/225g dried spaghetti
8 thin slices pepperoncini
1/2 lobster tail, cut into 4 slices with its shell on
2 sprigs basil
1/2 tablespoon chopped fresh parsley
2 tablespoons/30g unsalted butter
Salt and freshly ground black pepper to taste

1. Preheat the oven to 225°F/110°C. Line a baking sheet with aluminum foil and lightly brush with olive oil. Sprinkle the pan with the sea salt. Set aside.

2. In a medium saucepan, bring 1 quart/1 liter water to a boil. Meanwhile, with a paring knife, cut out the stems from the tomatoes and make a small "X" in the opposite ends. Plunge the tomatoes in the boiling water and leave them in just until the skins are loosened, 10 to 20 seconds. With a slotted spoon, remove the tomatoes and place them in a large bowl of cold water until cool enough to handle. Slip off the skins and cut the tomatoes in half lengthwise. Gently remove the seeds from the halves.

3. Place the lemon slices on the prepared baking sheet. Top each slice with a tomato half, skin side down, and a sprig thyme. Bake for 1 hour. Remove from the oven, tent with aluminum foil to keep warm, and set aside.

4. In a large saucepan, heat 1 tablespoon oil over medium heat. Add half the shallots and half the garlic and cook, stirring, until softened. Add 2 tablespoons wine and bring to a boil.

5. Add the mussels. Cover and steam for 2 minutes, shaking the pan occasionally. Begin checking the mussels; as they open, transfer them to a large bowl. Total steaming time will be about 4 minutes. Discard any mussels that do not open.

6. Strain the mussel broth through a fine sieve lined with cheesecloth into a small saucepan. Reserve. Repeat the procedure with the clams, using 2 tablespoons oil, and the remaining shallots, garlic, and wine, adding the shrimp and scallops at the end. Strain the clam broth into the mussel broth. Remove the mussels and clams from their shells and place in a small bowl with the shrimp and scallops. Set aside.

7. Cook the spaghetti in a stockpot of boiling salted water until al dente, 6 to 8 minutes. Drain and drizzle with a bit of olive oil to prevent sticking.

8. In a large saucepan, heat the remaining 1 tablespoon oil over medium-high heat. Add the pepperoncini and stir once. Immediately add the lobster medallions. Cook, stirring, until the seafood is half cooked, about 4 minutes. Add the reserved mussels, clams, shrimp, scallops, and their broth and bring to a boil. Add the spaghetti, reserved baked lemon, reserved tomatoes, basil, and parsley. Toss together thoroughly to combine. When all the ingredients are heated through, stir in the butter. Season with salt and pepper and serve immediately.

# Pan-Roasted Striped Bass in Oyster-Bean Sauce

Yield: 2 servings

## Oyster-Bean Sauce

5 tablespoons/75g unsalted butter, cut into
  cubes and chilled
1 clove garlic, finely chopped
2 teaspoons finely chopped fresh ginger
¼ cup/60ml fish stock

6 tablespoons fermented black and red beans
1 tablespoon sugar
2 tablespoons oyster sauce
  Fresh lemon juice to taste
  Salt and freshly ground black pepper to taste

In a heavy saucepan, melt 1 tablespoon/15g butter over low heat. Add the garlic and ginger and cook, stirring, until softened. Add the stock, beans, sugar, and oyster sauce. Stir to incorporate. Increase the heat to medium-high and bring to a boil. Simmer, stirring occasionally, until the liquid has reduced by one-third. Whisk in the remaining 4 tablespoons/60g butter, a bit at a time, until sauce thickens slightly. Return to a boil and then immediately remove from the heat. Season with lemon juice, salt, and pepper. Cover and keep warm.

## Roasted Bass

2 tablespoons/30g unsalted butter
¼ pound/120g pea shoots
  Salt and freshly ground black pepper to taste
2 tablespoons canola oil

Two 6-ounce/180g fillets wild bass, skin on
1 tablespoon chiffonade of fresh Thai basil
1 tablespoon julienne strips of serrano chile

1. In a medium skillet, melt the butter over medium heat. Add the pea shoots and cook, stirring, until just wilted. Season with salt and pepper. Transfer to paper towels to drain.

2. Preheat the oven to 350°F/180°C. In a large ovenproof heavy pan or cast-iron skillet, heat the oil over medium-high heat. Season the bass fillets on both sides with salt and pepper and place in the pan, skin side down. Just when the skin begins to turn golden, transfer the pan to the oven and roast until the bass is opaque in the center.

3. To serve, form a ring of pea shoots on each of 2 warmed plates. Spoon 2 tablespoons sauce around each ring. Top each ring with a bass fillet and sprinkle the plate with the basil and chile. Serve immediately.

## legumes

Legumes, including beans, have supplied the world with protein and sexual vigor since time began. Native Americans revered the many New World bean varieties, including black, kidney, pinto, and lima; ancient Latin writers referred to Europe's fava beans and chickpeas. Asians valued their native adzuki, mung, and soy beans—inventing tofu from the latter—and Africans brought black-eyed peas to the American South. The vitalizing tendency of legumes concerned Saint Jerome, the Croatian ascetic and scholar (A.D. 342–420), who forbade nuns to eat them for fear the sisters might begin to crave other bodily pleasures.
Like many lovers, beans perform their best when allowed to luxuriate in a long bath before cooking. Try combining them with grains for optimum protein balance and pepping them up with other aphrodisiacs like garlic and pepper for maximum effect.

# Pepper-Crusted Yellowfin Tuna with Papaya-Ginger Relish and Beet Chips

Y IELD : 2 SERVINGS

## Papaya-Ginger Relish

1 red papaya, peeled, seeded, and cut into
  ¼-inch/6mm dice
1 small red onion, minced
1 poblano chile, cut into julienne strips
2 tablespoons minced fresh ginger
2 tablespoons chiffonade of fresh cilantro

2 tablespoons extra-virgin olive oil
  Juice of 1 lime
1 tablespoon rice wine vinegar
  Grated zest of 1 orange
1 teaspoon ancho chile powder
  Salt and freshly ground black pepper to taste

In a medium bowl, combine all the ingredients. Stir to mix well. Cover and refrigerate for at least 2 hours to allow the flavors to blend. (Use the left-over relish with grilled chicken or pork.)

## Beet Chips

½ cup/125ml canola oil
1 red beet, peeled and cut into paper-thin slices
1 tablespoon cornstarch
  Salt and freshly ground black pepper to taste

In a heavy pan or cast-iron skillet, heat the oil to 350°F/180°C. (A small piece of bread dropped into the oil should float to the surface almost immediately and brown within 45 seconds.) Dust the beets with cornstarch and deep-fry in batches until golden brown, about 2 minutes. Drain on paper towels and lightly season with salt and pepper. Reserve.

## Tuna

Two 6-ounce/180g fillets sushi-grade yellowfin tuna
2 tablespoons canola oil
  Salt to taste
2 tablespoons coarsely ground black pepper

¼ pound/120g spinach, preferably flat-leaf, washed
  and stemmed
2 tablespoons basil oil (optional)

1. Lightly brush the tuna fillets with the oil and season with salt. Coat each fillet on all sides with 1 tablespoon black pepper. Heat a large heavy pan or cast-iron skillet over high heat until just smoking. Place the tuna in the pan and sear evenly on each side, keeping the inside rare. Transfer to a platter and let cool for 1 minute. Slice each fillet into 3 pieces.

2. To serve, divide the spinach leaves between 2 plates. Top with the tuna slices and papaya-ginger relish. Garnish with the beet chips and drizzle with basil oil if using.

## beets

Pliny the Elder, the Roman encyclopedist (A.D. 23–79), strongly advocated root vegetables and wrote that white beets in particular were "guaranteed to inflame the passions." Others attest that beets delay the aging process. Charlemagne, king of the Franks and emperor of the West (A.D. 742–814), ordered beets to be planted in his extensive domain, where both the greens and globe-shaped roots were consumed. The red variety was introduced to Europe in the sixteenth or seventeenth century. Boil some, and you may find that their crimson color and tender texture make your pulse race.

# Roasted Turbot with Baby Vegetables and Vermouth Sauce

Yield: 2 servings

## Vegetables

2  baby artichokes, trimmed and halved
4  baby turnips, peeled
2  radishes
4  pearl onions, peeled

2  scallions, white part only
8  haricots verts
16  fresh fava beans, from about 5 bean pods

1. Bring a large saucepan of salted water to a boil. Prepare a large bowl of ice water. Add the artichokes to the boiling water and boil until partially cooked, about 5 minutes. Remove the artichokes with a strainer and plunge them into the ice water to stop the cooking. Remove the artichokes from the ice water and place in a medium bowl.

2. Repeat this procedure with the turnips, radishes, pearl onions, scallions, and *haricots verts*, boiling each separately until partially cooked and then shocking in the ice water. Add the turnips, radishes, and pearl onions to the bowl with the artichokes. In another medium bowl, combine the scallions and *haricots verts*.

3. Add the fava beans to the still boiling water and boil for 30 seconds. Drain the beans and quickly plunge them into the ice water. When cold, remove them from the ice water and place them in a bowl. Using your fingernail, pinch open the tough outer covering of each bean and remove and discard it. Add the shucked beans to the scallions and *haricots verts*. Reserve.

## Turbot

4  tablespoons olive oil
Two 7- to 8-ounce/200 to 225g fillets turbot
Salt and freshly ground white pepper to taste

¼  cup/60ml dry vermouth
2  tablespoons chicken stock
1  stick/120g unsalted butter, cut into small pieces

1. In a large skillet, heat 2 tablespoons oil over medium-high heat. Season the turbot fillets with salt and white pepper and add to the pan. Sauté the turbot on both sides until beginning to turn golden but not cooked through. Transfer the fillets to a warmed large platter and tent with aluminum foil to keep warm.

2. In the same skillet, heat the remaining 2 tablespoons oil over medium-high heat. Add the reserved artichokes, turnips, radishes, and pearl onions. Cook, stirring, until the onions just begin to turn golden. Add the vermouth and reduce the liquid by two-thirds. Add the stock and bring to a boil. Add the butter and stir until a sauce consistency forms. Add the scallions, *haricots verts*, fava beans, and reserved turbot. Simmer gently, covered, until the fish and vegetables are cooked through.

3. To serve, transfer the fish to a clean warmed platter and tent with foil to keep warm. Season the sauce and vegetables with salt and white pepper. Divide the vegetables between 2 warmed plates and place the fillets on top. Spoon the sauce around the fillets and serve immediately.

## mushrooms

These fungi are mysterious. They sprout after a soft rain like . . . well . . . like mushrooms. There are tens of thousands of varieties growing in the dark forest among witches, fawns, and fairies. Brushing away the dirt reveals a pale flesh as smooth and supple as a woman's. Wild mushrooms pose even greater mystery, for the differences between the highly poisonous and the edible are subtle indeed. (Forage for yours at the market, please.) Mushrooms contain some potassium and phosphorus, but the most important element they bring to the table is their earthy sensuality. Although Western scientists once attributed humans with the capacity to taste four distinct flavors, many now believe we have the ability to detect a fifth flavor—a savory earthiness found in foods such as mushrooms and meat. Conduct a bit of your own research *chez vous*, with portobellos, porcini, enoki, and chanterelles.

# Sautéed Red Snapper with Wild Mushrooms and Asparagus

YIELD: 2 SERVINGS

### Mushroom Sauce

4 tablespoons/60g unsalted butter
½ onion, diced
1 stalk celery, diced
½ carrot, diced

½ bunch fresh thyme, leaves chopped
2 cloves garlic, coarsely chopped
¼ pound/120g fresh crimini mushrooms, sliced
1 cup/250ml chicken stock

In a large saucepan, melt the butter over medium-high heat. Add everything except the stock. Cook, stirring, until the vegetables soften, 3 to 4 minutes.

Add the stock and bring to a boil. Reduce the heat and simmer for 1 hour, or until reduced by two-thirds. Strain through a fine sieve and keep warm.

### Mushrooms and Asparagus

4 tablespoons/60g unsalted butter, clarified (see technique, page 14)
2 ounces/60g fresh oyster mushrooms

2 ounces/60g fresh shiitake mushrooms
2 ounces/60g fresh porcini mushrooms
8 spears asparagus

1. In a large skillet, heat about one-third of the butter over medium heat. Add the oyster mushrooms and cook, stirring, until evenly browned. Transfer to a large colander placed over a bowl and drain. Repeat with the shiitake mushrooms and then the porcini mushrooms, each time transferring them to the colander with the oyster mushrooms to drain. Set aside.

2. Bring a large saucepan of salted water to a boil. Prepare a large bowl of ice water. Pare down the base of any large asparagus spears with a vegetable peeler to remove the fibrous outer layer. Place the asparagus in the boiling water and cook until just tender but still bright green. Drain immediately and shock in the ice water. Drain and cut the asparagus into 2-inch/5cm lengths. Set aside.

### Red Snapper

2 tablespoons olive oil
Two 6-ounce/180g fillets red snapper, skin on
Salt and freshly ground black pepper to taste

1 tablespoon/15g unsalted butter
Parsley sprigs and tomato wedges for garnish

1. In a large skillet, heat the oil over medium-high heat. Season the snapper fillets on both sides with salt and pepper and place in the skillet, skin side down. Cook until the snapper just turns opaque in the center. Transfer to a warmed platter and tent with aluminum foil to keep warm.

2. Meanwhile, in a large skillet, melt the butter over medium heat. Add the reserved mushrooms

and asparagus and cook, tossing occasionally, until heated through. Add the mushroom sauce and reduce slightly. Season with salt and pepper.

3. To serve, spoon the mushroom mixture and sauce on each of 2 warmed plates. Top with the red snapper, garnish with parsley and tomato wedges, and serve immediately.

# Sea Scallop Seviche

YIELD: 2 SERVINGS

### Salad

*Grated zest of ½ lemon*
*Grated zest of ½ lime*
2 *tablespoons fresh lemon juice*
1 *tablespoon fresh lime juice*
¼ *cup/60ml chile oil (optional)*
*Salt to taste*
*Pinch cayenne pepper*

1 *ripe medium tomato*
½ *red bell pepper, cored, seeded, and finely diced*
1 *scallion, thinly sliced*
½ *shallot, thinly sliced*
1 *tablespoon chopped fresh cilantro*
½ *tablespoon finely chopped fresh chives*

1. In a small bowl, combine the lemon zest, lime zest, lemon juice, and lime juice. Whisk in the chile oil if using. Season with salt and cayenne. Set aside.

2. In a small saucepan, bring 1 quart/1 liter water to a boil. Meanwhile, with a paring knife, cut out the stem from the tomato and make a small "X" in the opposite end. Plunge the tomato in the boiling water and leave it in just until the skin is loosened, 10 to 20 seconds. With a slotted spoon, remove the tomato and rinse it under cold water until cool enough to handle. Slip off the skin and cut the tomato in half. Gently but firmly squeeze the seeds from the tomato halves and dice.

3. In a medium bowl, combine the diced tomatoes, bell pepper, scallion, shallot, cilantro, and chives. Add the lemon-lime mixture and toss. Cover with plastic wrap and let the vegetables marinate in the refrigerator for 12 hours.

## Scallops

2 cups/500ml water
½ cup/125ml dry white wine
½ onion, cut into ½-inch/1.25cm-thick slices
½ carrot, cut into ½-inch/1.25cm-thick slices
1 stalk celery, cut into ½-inch/1.25cm-thick slices
5 black peppercorns, finely crushed
3 coriander seeds
½ pound large sea scallops

1. In a large saucepan, combine all the ingredients except the scallops. Bring to a boil over high heat. Reduce the heat and simmer for 20 minutes. Strain through a fine sieve into a wide saucepan.

2. Return the broth to a simmer and add the scallops. Cook until poached but still rare in the middle, about 2 minutes. With a slotted spoon, quickly transfer the scallops to a bowl. Let cool to room temperature. Cover with plastic wrap and chill until needed.

## Avocado Puree

2 Haas avocados, cut in half lengthwise, peeled, and pitted
Juice of ½ lemon
Juice of 1 lime
½ cup/125ml crème fraîche (page 8) or sour cream
Tabasco sauce to taste
Salt to taste

1. Coarsely dice the avocados. Place in a food processor and puree until smooth. Add the remaining ingredients and puree until combined.

2. To serve, divide the chilled scallops between 2 plates. Top with the salad. Garnish with the avocado puree. Serve immediately.

# Crayfish with Tomato and Garlic Sauce

YIELD: 2 SERVINGS

2 tablespoons olive oil
½ medium carrot, diced
½ small onion, diced
1 stalk celery, diced
1 pound/454g peeled crayfish
1 tablespoon cognac
1 cup/250ml crushed tomatoes
¼ cup/60ml dry white wine

1 clove garlic, chopped
1 teaspoon chopped fresh thyme
1 teaspoon chopped fresh marjoram
1 teaspoon chopped fresh parsley
1 bay leaf
   Salt and freshly ground black pepper to taste
1 teaspoon chopped fresh cilantro

1. In a heavy saucepan, heat the oil over high heat. Add the carrot, onion, and celery. Reduce the heat to low and cook, stirring, until the onion is translucent but not browned, 5 to 7 minutes.

2. Add the crayfish and cook, stirring, for 3 minutes. Add the cognac and scrape up any browned bits from the bottom of the pan. Cook, stirring, for 3 minutes. Add all the remaining ingredients except the cilantro and stir until combined. With the heat still on low, cover and cook for 10 minutes.

3. To serve, divide the crayfish mixture between 2 warmed plates. Sprinkle with the cilantro and serve with fresh pasta.

## crayfish

Like most crustaceans, crayfish have a racy reputation, especially in the Mediterranean region. The French have mastered *soupe d'écrevisse*, a hearty, highly spiced crayfish soup whose effects have been compared to those of the famed bird's nest soup, created thousands of miles away in China. It was probably the French who spread the word in southern Louisiana, where folks boil their "crawfish" with enough red pepper to burn the lips and make the eyes water—a sure sign of love. First, twist off the critter's tail, then quickly sip the savory juice from the body shell; now you know the meaning of the Louisiana slogan "Suck the heads."

# Louisiana Oyster Pie

Yield: 4 servings

### Pie Shell

1 ½ cups/180g all-purpose flour
¼ teaspoon salt
8 tablespoons/120g vegetable shortening, chilled

3 to 4 tablespoons ice water
1 large egg white, beaten with 1 tablespoon water

1. In a large bowl, combine the flour and salt. Using your fingertips, work the shortening into the flour until the mixture resembles coarse meal. Add the water, stirring with a fork until the mixture forms a dough. Pat into a ball and chill, covered with plastic wrap, for at least 1 hour or up to 3 days.

2. Preheat the oven to 425°F/220°C. On a lightly floured surface, roll out the dough into a ⅛-inch/3mm-thick round. Drape the dough over a rolling pin and fit it into a 10-inch/25cm pie pan. Fold the edges under and crimp. Place the pie shell in the freezer for 20 minutes. Remove the shell and prick it all over with the tines of a fork to prevent bubbling during baking.

3. Place a piece of aluminum foil over the dough and fill it with pie weights or beans. Place the shell in the oven and bake for 6 minutes. Remove the foil and brush the sides and bottom of the shell with the egg white wash. Return to the oven and bake an additional 8 to 10 minutes. Place on a wire rack and let cool before filling.

### Oyster Filling

1 bunch watercress
2 tablespoons/30g unsalted butter
3 tablespoons chopped shallots
½ teaspoon chopped garlic
1 cup/345g coarsely chopped cooked spinach
2 tablespoons Pernod

Salt and freshly ground black pepper to taste
3 dozen oysters, freshly shucked, juice reserved
½ cup/125ml heavy cream
1 large egg
2 tablespoons grated Parmesan cheese
Grated nutmeg to taste

1. Preheat the oven to 325°F/160°C. Bring a large saucepan of salted water to a boil. Cut the stems off the watercress and chop the leaves coarsely. Add to the pan and blanch for 2 minutes. Remove with a sieve and drain thoroughly.

2. In a skillet, melt the butter over low heat. Add the shallots and garlic and cook, stirring, until transparent. Add the watercress, spinach, and Pernod. Cook, stirring, until heated through. Season with salt and pepper. Set aside.

3. In a small saucepan, heat the oysters with their juice over medium heat. Without bringing them to a boil, cook the oysters just until firm, 2 minutes.

4. Spread the watercress mixture in the bottom of the prepared pie shell. Top with the oysters. In a small bowl, whisk the cream, egg, and Parmesan until combined. Season with salt, pepper, and nutmeg. Pour the egg mixture over the watercress and oysters.

5. Place the pie in the oven and bake for 25 minutes, or until lightly browned and set. Let cool for a few minutes before cutting into wedges.

# Linguine with Clams, Pancetta, and Grilled Leeks

1 large leek, white part only, cut in half
2 tablespoons olive oil
 Salt and freshly ground white pepper to taste
2 ounces/60g pancetta, diced
½ pound/225g dried linguine
2 cloves garlic, minced
1 shallot, minced
 Zest of 1 lemon, blanched and finely chopped

1 pound/454g clams (small littlenecks or cockles), scrubbed well under cold water
1 ½ cups/375ml dry white wine
 Juice of ½ lemon
 Pinch crushed red pepper
1 tablespoon/15g unsalted butter
1 tablespoon chopped fresh parsley
1 tablespoon chopped fresh basil plus 2 whole leaves for garnish

## clams

Japanese folklore instructs men and women to bake clams until completely hardened, then to pulverize them into a powder. A tiny dose of this powder with water every night for a week, two hours before bedtime, is supposed to restore sexual vitality. Most of us would rather steam or fry our clams or add them to chowder. Freshly harvested littlenecks, cherrystones, and pismos are best slurped raw from the shell—held gently to your lips by the hand of your mate. Conduct your own research on other bivalve mollusks, such as scallops and mussels, rumored to arouse similar vim.

1. Heat a charcoal grill. Lightly coat the leek with some of the olive oil. Season with salt and white pepper. Grill the leek until well marked but not burned. (Alternatively, you may use the broiler.) Let cool and cut into julienne strips. Set aside.

2. In a small skillet over medium heat, cook the pancetta, stirring, until the fat is rendered, about 10 minutes. Drain the pancetta and set aside.

3. Cook the linguine in a stockpot of boiling salted water until al dente, 6 to 8 minutes. Drain and drizzle with a bit of the olive oil to prevent sticking. Set aside.

4. In a large skillet, heat the remaining olive oil over medium heat. Add the garlic, shallot, lemon zest, and leeks. Cook, stirring, until the shallot is almost softened, approximately 2 minutes.

5. Add the clams, wine, and pancetta. Cover and steam for 3 to 4 minutes, shaking the skillet occasionally. Begin checking the clams; as they open, transfer them to a serving bowl and keep warm. Discard any clams that do not open.

6. Simmer the clam broth until reduced by half. Add the lemon juice and crushed red pepper. Whisk in the butter and reduce slightly. Season with salt and white pepper.

7. To serve, stir the cooked linguine into the sauce and toss to coat. Add the parsley and chopped basil and toss again. Divide the linguine between 2 large plates. Arrange the clams around the linguine and garnish with the whole basil leaves. Serve immediately.

# Spicy Clams with Green Sauce

YIELD: 2 SERVINGS

32  littleneck clams, scrubbed well under cold water
4  tablespoons/60g unsalted butter, clarified
   (see technique, page 14)
1  tablespoon finely chopped garlic
¼  cup/30g finely chopped scallions
¼  cup/60ml plus 1 tablespoon dry white wine

¾  cup/200ml canned clam juice
⅛  teaspoon crushed red pepper
1  tablespoon arrowroot or cornstarch
   Salt and freshly ground black pepper to taste
¼  cup/5g chopped fresh parsley

1. In a large skillet, heat the butter over medium-high heat. When it is very hot, add the garlic, sauté for a few seconds, then add the clams. Increase the heat to high and cook, stirring, for about 30 seconds. Add the scallions, ¼ cup/60ml wine, clam juice, and crushed red pepper. Bring to a boil for approximately 4 minutes until the clams open. Discard any clams that do not open. Remove the clams and set aside. Bring the liquid again to a boil, this time over medium heat.

2. In a small bowl, quickly blend the remaining 1 tablespoon wine with the arrowroot or cornstarch. Stir this mixture into the liquid in the skillet and cook, stirring constantly, until the liquid is thickened. Season with salt and pepper. Place the clams back into the skillet, and cook for another 30 seconds. Divide this generous portion between 2 soup plates, sprinkle with parsley, and serve with either rice or garlic bread, accompanied by a nice dry white wine.

## parsley

It's not just a garnish anymore. Parsley, whether tightly curled or flat, adds a bit of bliss to soups, sauces, salads, and other dishes. And what sour spouse would ever dream that you were so cunning as to slip a little *fun* into those dumplings? This aphrodisiac, once considered a merely decorative plant before even arriving at garnish status, is also an excellent breath freshener, so munch on a few sprigs while doing the dishes.

# Poached Salmon with Saffron Sauce

YIELD: 2 SERVINGS

2 ½ cups/625ml fish stock
½ teaspoon sea salt
1 bay leaf, crumbled
5 whole white peppercorns
Two 6- to 8-ounce/180 to 225g fillets salmon
½ cup/125ml dry white wine
1 shallot, finely chopped

½ cup/125ml heavy cream
½ teaspoon saffron threads
3 tablespoons/45g unsalted butter, cut into small pieces and chilled
Salt and freshly ground white pepper to taste
6 large spinach leaves
2 teaspoons salmon caviar (optional)

1. In a large skillet with high sides, combine 2 cups/500ml stock, the sea salt, bay leaf, and peppercorns. Bring to a simmer over medium heat. Add the salmon in a single layer and poach until it just turns opaque in the center. Transfer the salmon to 2 warmed plates and tent with aluminum foil to keep warm.

2. In a medium nonreactive saucepan, combine the wine, shallot, and remaining ½ cup/125ml stock. Bring to a boil over medium heat and reduce the liquid to only 2 tablespoons. Add the cream and return to a boil; reduce by half. Strain the sauce through a fine sieve into a smaller saucepan. Add the saffron and return to a boil. Remove from the heat and whisk in the butter. Season with salt and white pepper and keep warm over low heat.

3. Preheat the oven to 350°F/180°C. Meanwhile, place the spinach in a steamer and steam until wilted. Spread 3 overlapping leaves on a platter, top with a salmon fillet, and fold the edges up and over as if wrapping a package. Repeat. Reheat the wrapped salmon fillets in the oven for approximately 4 minutes.

4. To serve, swirl some sauce on 2 warmed dinner plates. Invert the spinach-wrapped salmon fillets on the sauce, and spoon some caviar on top if using. Serve immediately.

## saffron

If the stigmas of flowers are the sex organs of plants, as a green-thumbed wise man once told me, then it is no wonder that saffron has the tendency to set the stage for a stimulating evening. This spice is actually the golden orange stigma of the purple autumn crocus. Ancient Greeks believed that a woman who ate saffron every day for one week would be unable to resist her lover's charms, and recent experiments lead some scientists to believe it has a similar effect on rats and mice. A wee quantity of saffron lends any dish a lovely golden hue, especially pleasing in Spanish rice, bouillabaisse, and cakes.

As 14,000 stigmas must be hand-picked to make a single ounce, saffron is the most expensive spice in the world. And like many spices, saffron in excessive amounts is toxic. Don't worry. With just a tiny pinch, you'll have flavor, color, and a lover who cannot untie your apron fast enough.

# Grilled Salmon Steak
# with Pernod

*2 tablespoons olive oil*
*1 clove garlic, minced*
*2 tablespoons chopped tomato*
*2 tablespoons Pernod*
*1 teaspoon chopped fresh thyme*

*1 bay leaf*
*Pinch salt*
*1 tablespoon chopped fresh parsley*
*Two 8-ounce/225g salmon steaks, tiny bones removed*

1. In a medium skillet, heat the oil over medium-high heat. Add the garlic and tomato; cook, stirring, for 4 to 5 minutes. Add the Pernod and stir until incorporated. Add the thyme, bay leaf, salt, and parsley. Continue cooking until thickened. Remove from the heat, transfer to a container, cover, and chill in the refrigerator for 30 to 45 minutes. Discard the bay leaf.

2. Heat a charcoal grill to a medium temperature. Lightly coat 2 large squares of aluminum foil with olive oil. Place a piece of salmon steak in the center of each square. Spoon 2 tablespoons garlic-tomato mixture on top of each piece of salmon. Wrap the salmon in the foil, sealing the ends.

3. Place the foil packages on the grill and cook for 5 to 6 minutes on each side. (Alternatively, you may use the broiler or bake in the oven.) Transfer to warmed plates and carefully remove the salmon from the foil. Serve immediately.

## licorice

You either pick the black jelly beans from the candy dish straightaway, or you ignore them and hope your spouse (or maybe the neighbor's children) will eat them. Licorice, either loved or hated, always inspires passionate feelings. The perennial herb has been a component of medicines from Asia to northern Africa and Europe since ancient times. It is also a flavor component in liqueurs such as Pernod and absinthe. Vatsayana included it in several beverages in the *Kama Sutra* recommended to increase sexual inclination. In very high doses licorice can raise blood pressure. Then again, so can slowly undressing each other.

## fish

Erotologists, experts in love and sex, have had a fondness for fish since ancient times. Nearly every culture has idolized the fish, not only as a food but also as a symbol of life. Although all fish contain high-quality protein, phosphorus, and iodine, nutrients known to rev up the libido, I have noticed that those most frequently cited for stimulating desire are distinctive-tasting, fatty fish such as anchovies, eel, herring, salmon, sardines, tuna, and trout. But don't get me wrong. I tend to think that a lovingly prepared dinner of lean fish such as cod, flounder, or halibut will also have your partner nuzzling your neck. The Egyptians so adamantly believed fish to be sexually stimulating that they forbade their priests from partaking at all. Ancient Roman women ate trout to prepare for meetings with their inexhaustible husbands. The French still follow the lead of Henry IV of France (1533–1610), whose chef kept a potful of sautéed eel hot on the stove all day in case the king needed to fortify himself before an amorous encounter.

# Sliced Salmon with Mustard Sauce

YIELD: 2 SERVINGS

### Mustard Sauce

2 tablespoons prepared mayonnaise
1 tablespoon prepared old-fashioned whole-grain mustard
½ tablespoon chopped fresh chives
2 drops fresh lemon juice
Salt and freshly ground black pepper to taste

In a small bowl, combine the mayonnaise, mustard, chives, and lemon juice. Season with salt and pepper. Cover and chill in the refrigerator until needed.

### Salmon

Salt and freshly ground black pepper to taste
Two 6-ounce/180g pieces fresh salmon, thinly sliced
4 baguette slices, lightly brushed with olive oil and toasted

2 sprigs parsley
2 small cherry tomatoes
½ medium cucumber, peeled and thinly sliced

1. Preheat the broiler on medium until very hot. Sprinkle a baking sheet with salt and pepper and lay the salmon on it. Broil for 30 seconds, or until slightly medium-rare. With a spatula, transfer the salmon to a cold baking sheet and cover with plastic wrap. Chill in the refrigerator until cold.

2. To serve, spread 1 tablespoon mustard sauce on each of 2 plates. Top with the salmon. Garnish each plate with 2 baguette croutons, a parsley sprig, a cherry tomato, and a few slices of cucumber. Serve with fresh lemon or topped with salmon caviar if desired. This can be also served hot.

# Crab Cakes with Ginger Dressing and Watercress

YIELD: 2 SERVINGS

## Crab Cakes

2 tablespoons/30g unsalted butter

2 tablespoons finely chopped white onion

1 clove garlic, finely chopped

2 tablespoons finely diced red bell pepper

2 tablespoons finely diced green bell pepper

2 tablespoons finely diced yellow bell pepper

½ pound/225g lump crabmeat, picked over for shells

1 tablespoon prepared mayonnaise

⅓ cup/50g fresh bread crumbs

Salt and freshly ground black pepper to taste

1. In a medium skillet, melt the butter over high heat. Add the onion and garlic and cook, stirring, until softened but not colored, about 2 minutes. Add the bell peppers. Cook, stirring, until the peppers are softened, 5 minutes more. Remove from the heat and let cool.

2. Transfer the vegetables to a medium bowl. Add the crabmeat, mayonnaise, and bread crumbs. Mix gently and season with salt and pepper. Cover with plastic wrap and chill in the refrigerator for 2 to 3 hours.

## Ginger Dressing

1 large egg

¼ cup/35g chopped yellow onion

3 ½ tablespoons grated fresh ginger

1 ½ tablespoons honey

1 teaspoon salt

½ teaspoon Dijon mustard

¼ teaspoon coarsely ground black pepper

Pinch cayenne pepper

1 ¼ cups/310ml vegetable oil

⅓ cup/75ml cider vinegar

In a food processor, combine all the ingredients except the oil and vinegar. Process for 30 seconds. With the motor running, very slowly add the oil and vinegar in alternating increments. When a creamy consistency is reached, transfer the dressing to a bowl; cover and chill until ready to use.

## watercress

The peppery spice of this freshwater green probably tipped off the English to its aphrodisiac powers. Pair it with other salad greens if you are unaccustomed to its hot bite, or contrast it against lush citrus fruits and pears. Watercress scores high points for vitamin C, beta-carotene, and its cool, bracing character, which you can tone down by steaming it or spreading it over simmering soup just before serving. Look for a new glint in your mate's eye before bringing out the entree.

## Tomato Concassé

*1 ripe medium tomato*
*½ tablespoon whole-grain mustard*

*1 teaspoon chopped fresh chives*
*Water or white wine, if needed*

1. In a medium saucepan, bring 4 cups/1 liter water to a boil. Meanwhile, with a paring knife, cut out the stem from the tomato and make a small "X" in the opposite end. Plunge the tomato in the boiling water and leave it in just until the skin is loosened, 10 to 20 seconds. With a slotted spoon, remove the tomato and rinse it under cold water until cool enough to handle. Slip off the skin and cut the tomato in half. Gently but firmly squeeze the seeds from the tomato halves. Dice the tomato.

2. In a small saucepan, combine the diced tomato, mustard, and chives over medium heat. Stir until warmed through. Add some water or white wine if it becomes too dry. Keep warm.

## To Assemble

*2 tablespoons vegetable oil*
*¼ pound/120g watercress*
*2 tablespoons finely diced red bell pepper*

*2 tablespoons finely diced green bell pepper*
*2 tablespoons finely diced yellow bell pepper*

1. Preheat the oven to 200°F/95°C and place a baking sheet in it. Form the crab cake mixture into 2 patties. In a large skillet, heat the oil over high heat. Sauté the crab cakes until golden, about 4 minutes per side.

2. To serve, prepare a bed of watercress on each of 2 plates. Place a mound of tomato concassé in the center of each plate and top with a crab cake. Spoon the ginger dressing around the plate and sprinkle with the bell peppers. Serve immediately.

# Lobster Steak Topped with Fried Egg

YIELD: 2 SERVINGS

## Lobster Curry Oil

*Head and claws of 1 lobster*
*(see "Lobster Steaks" below)*

*¼ cup/60ml olive oil*
*1 tablespoon curry oil*

Prepare the oil a day in advance. Chop the head and claws into small pieces. Place in a food processor and pulse until they are broken down further. Warm a skillet over the stove, then add the oil. Sauté the lobster pieces in the oil for 3 minutes. Remove from the heat, then stir in the curry. Refrigerate overnight and strain before using.

## Lobster Steaks

*1 pound/454g lobster meat (from three 1 ½-pound/680g lobsters), cut into large pieces (reserve head and claws)*
*2 large egg whites*
*3 tablespoons/45g unsalted butter, softened*

*Salt and freshly ground white pepper to taste*
*2 tablespoons canola oil*
*2 large eggs*
*2 tablespoons/30g unsalted butter or oil*

1. Lightly butter a baking sheet and two 3 ½-inch /8.75cm pastry rings. Place the rings on the baking sheet and set aside.

2. In a food processor, chop the lobster meat into smaller pieces. Add the egg whites and butter. Season with salt and white pepper. Process until the mixture just comes together and there are still large pieces of lobster in the mix. Spoon the mixture into the prepared pastry rings on the baking sheet and cover with plastic wrap. Chill in the refrigerator until firm.

3. In a medium skillet, heat the oil over medium heat. Remove the lobster steaks from their rings and add to the skillet. Cook until lightly golden on the bottom. Flip and cook until opaque in the center, 3 to 4 minutes on each side. Reserve.

4. Break the eggs into a bowl without damaging the yolks. Heat the butter or oil in a skillet until it is very hot; slide the eggs into the skillet and reduce the heat to medium-low. Fry the eggs until the egg whites have set, about 1 minute. Tilt the skillet and allow the butter or oil to collect at the side of the skillet.

5. To serve, top each lobster steak with a sunny-side-up fried egg. Garnish the plate with the lobster curry oil.

# Roasted Lobster
# with Tarragon-Basil Butter

YIELD: 2 SERVINGS

1 stick/120g unsalted butter, softened

1 teaspoon finely chopped fresh basil

1 teaspoon finely chopped fresh cilantro

1 teaspoon finely chopped fresh tarragon

2 teaspoons finely chopped fresh parsley

2 cloves garlic, finely chopped

1 shallot, finely chopped

2 tablespoons cognac

1 tablespoon dry white wine

1 tablespoon champagne vinegar

½ teaspoon Dijon mustard

Two 1 ½-pound/680g lobsters, freshly killed

1. Preheat the oven to 350°F/180°C. In a food processor fitted with a whip attachment, combine all the ingredients except the lobster. Whip until smooth. Set aside 2 generous tablespoons of the herb butter, cover, and chill in the refrigerator. Place the remainder in a pastry bag fitted with a medium round tip.

2. With a sharpening steel or some other type of round heavy-duty rod, pierce the head of each lobster. Pipe the herb butter into the hole in each lobster's head until you can see the butter proceeding toward the end of the tail.

3. Place the lobsters on a baking sheet and roast in the oven for 12 minutes. Remove them from the oven. Place the lobsters on their backs on a cutting board and cut in half lengthwise. Crack open the claws. Place each lobster on its back on a baking sheet. Cover the lobster meat with the chilled herb butter and return to the oven for 2 to 3 minutes. Divide between 2 plates and serve immediately.

# lobster

Picture dancer Josephine Baker (1906–75) reclining nude in her Paris dressing room, eating lobster, a favorite food of expatriate Americans in the 1920s, and drinking champagne. There is nothing like watching the one you love hungrily attack a boiled lobster, breaking open the claws with a nutcracker, licking the juices from each finger, one at a time. Gourmets insist on Maine lobsters; if these are unavailable, try spiny or Pacific rock. In the underwater kingdom and in the realm of aphrodisiacs, lobsters are very similar to crayfish, their smaller, freshwater crustacean cousins. Lobster is high in protein and minerals to boost your sex drive, including phosphorus, calcium, and potassium. For the best flavor and erotic effect, select lively specimens from the market or restaurant tank. The greenish blue beasts will blush bright red when boiled, as you might when your mate gets you home.

# Lobster Risotto

YIELD: 4 SERVINGS

6 cups/1.5l chicken or lobster stock
½ cup/1.25ml olive oil
2 tablespoons/30g unsalted butter
¼ cup/35g finely chopped onion
½ sprig chopped rosemary, plus 2 ¼ whole sprigs

1 cup/200g Arborio rice
¼ cup/60ml dry white wine
2 lobster tails, cooked, shelled, and diced
1 cup/100g freshly grated Parmesan cheese
Salt and freshly ground black pepper to taste

1. In a medium saucepan, bring the stock to a boil. Reduce the heat and hold at a simmer.

2. Meanwhile, in a medium cast-iron skillet, heat the oil and ½ tablespoon butter over medium-low heat. Add the onion and chopped rosemary and cook, stirring, until the onion is softened, about 2 minutes. Add the rice and stir with a wooden spoon until well coated, about 4 minutes.

3. Add the wine and cook, stirring, until the liquid evaporates. Slowly add enough stock to cover the rice, about 1 cup/250ml. Simmer, stirring continuously, until the liquid is almost absorbed. Add another cup of stock and cook, stirring, until almost absorbed. Continue to add stock, 1 cup/250ml at a time, until the risotto has cooked for a total of 15 minutes and is creamy but still slightly firm in the center.

4. Add the lobster, the remaining 1 ½ tablespoons butter, and the Parmesan. Cook, stirring, until the lobster is heated through, 1 to 2 minutes more. Season with salt and pepper.

5. Serve the risotto in warmed bowls. Garnish with the whole rosemary sprigs.

# chile peppers

## (Capsicums)

Christopher Columbus mistook capsicums for the rare spice he sought in the New World, dubbing them "peppers." The misnomer persists to this day. These fleshy pods contain capsaicin, the incendiary chemical that gives them "heat" and makes you want to laugh, cry, and make love—all at the same time. The Aztecs of Mexico and the Arawaks of the Caribbean used capsicums extensively; the Spanish and Portuguese took note and brought them to Europe, Asia, and Africa, where they caught on and now play an integral part in cooking and culture. What happens when you and your lover bite into these charmers? First, the pain detectors in your lips, mouth, throat and nose get riled up, sending stimulating "danger" messages to the brain. The brain reacts by releasing endorphins—morphinelike hormones—which provide a rush of pleasurable relief and a sense of euphoria. Are these aphrodisiacs addictive? You bet, and as with sensational sex, the more you have, the more you want.

# Grilled Lobsters with Serrano Chile Butter

2  tablespoons dry white wine
2  serrano chiles, seeded and finely chopped
1  medium shallot, finely chopped
1  teaspoon crushed red peppercorns
1  tablespoon heavy cream
1  stick/120g unsalted butter, softened to
   room temperature

Salt and freshly ground black pepper to taste
Fresh lemon juice to taste
Two 1 ½-pound/680g lobsters
2  tablespoons olive oil
½  ripe tomato, seeded and diced
2  tablespoons finely chopped fresh basil
Parsley sprigs for garnish

I. In a small saucepan, combine the wine, chiles, shallot, and crushed peppercorns. Bring to a boil over medium heat. Reduce the heat and simmer, stirring, until almost dry. Add the cream and simmer, stirring, for 2 minutes more. Do not allow the mixture to burn.

2. Transfer the cream mixture to a food processor or blender; puree until smooth. Strain the mixture through a fine sieve into a medium bowl. Incorporate the butter slowly, mixing to combine. Season with salt, pepper, and lemon juice. Cover and chill in the refrigerator until ready to serve.

3. Heat a charcoal grill to a very high heat. Carefully grab each lobster by the tail and push the tip of a large sharp knife between its eyes to kill it instantly. (A fishmonger can do this for you.) Place the lobsters, back side down, on a cutting board and cut in half lengthwise. Flatten the lobsters slightly and remove the stomach and veins.

4. Brush the lobsters with the olive oil and grill, meat side down, for 7 to 8 minutes. Turn over and grill for about 5 minutes more. (Alternatively, roast the lobsters in a 420°F/215°C oven for 12 minutes.)

5. To serve, crack open the claws of the lobsters. Place each lobster, belly side up, on the plate. Top each with a dollop of chile butter. Sprinkle with the tomato, basil, and parsley.

# Tiger Prawns with Cucumber-Mango Salad

YIELD: 2 SERVINGS

## Cucumber-Mango Salad

1 cucumber, peeled, seeded, and cut into julienne strips
1 mango, peeled, pitted, and cut into julienne strips
1 red bell pepper, cored, seeded, and cut into julienne strips
1 yellow bell pepper, cored, seeded, and cut into julienne strips

3 scallions, both white and green parts, finely chopped
Grated zest of 2 limes
Grated zest of 3 lemons
1 shallot, minced
1 clove garlic, minced

In a medium bowl, combine the ingredients and reserve.

## Prawns

4 jumbo tiger prawns or 8 jumbo prawns
Salt and freshly ground black pepper to taste

1 tablespoon olive oil

1. Peel and devein the prawns, leaving the heads on. Remove the coral from the heads and reserve it for use in the vinaigrette.

2. Season the prawns with salt and pepper. In a cast-iron skillet, heat the oil over medium-high heat. Add the prawns and cook on both sides, 4 to 6 minutes, until opaque. Reserve.

## Citrus Vinaigrette

1 lime, peeled, cut into segments, and chopped
2 lemons, peeled, cut into segments, and chopped
½ cup/125ml olive oil

Dash cider vinegar
Salt and freshly ground black pepper to taste

In a small saucepan, combine the lime and lemon segments over medium-low heat. Whisk in the oil, vinegar, and reserved coral from the prawns. Season with salt and pepper. Remove from the heat. (The vinaigrette should be warm, not hot.) Reserve.

## To Assemble

2 leaves Boston or Bibb lettuce
1 tablespoon chopped fresh cilantro

1 tablespoon chopped fresh mint
Salt and freshly ground black pepper to taste

Place a piece of lettuce on each of 2 plates. Add the cilantro and mint to the cucumber-mango salad. Season with salt and pepper and divide between the lettuce leaves. Top the salad with the prawns. Dress with the warm vinaigrette and serve.

# Sautéed Flamed Shrimp

1  *ripe medium tomato*
3  *tablespoons/45g unsalted butter*
1  *small shallot, chopped*
¼  *bulb fennel, diced*
½  *red bell pepper, cored, seeded, and diced*
½  *cup sliced fresh white mushrooms*
¼  *cup/60ml heavy cream*

3  *cloves garlic, chopped*
2  *tablespoons chopped fresh parsley*
1  *pound/454g medium shrimp, peeled and deveined*
    *(approximately 20)*
    *Salt and freshly ground black pepper to taste*
¼  *cup/60ml cognac*
1  *tablespoon slivered almonds, toasted*

1. In a small saucepan, bring 2 cups/500ml water to a boil. Meanwhile, with a paring knife, cut out the stem from the tomato and make a small "X" in the opposite end. Plunge the tomato in the boiling water and leave it in just until the skin is loosened, 10 to 20 seconds. With a slotted spoon, remove the tomato and rinse it under cold water until cool enough to handle. Slip off the skin and cut the tomato in half. Gently but firmly squeeze the seeds from the tomato halves. Chop coarsely.

2. In a large skillet, melt 1 ½ tablespoons butter over medium heat. Add the shallot, fennel, and bell pepper. Cook, stirring, until lightly browned. Add the chopped tomato and mushrooms and cook, stirring, until the mushrooms soften. Add the cream and remove from the heat. Add the garlic and parsley and keep warm over low heat on the stove.

3. In another skillet, melt the remaining 1 ½ tablespoons butter over medium-high heat. Season the shrimp with salt and pepper and add them to the skillet. Cook, stirring, until the shrimp turn pink, about 2 minutes.

4. While carefully standing back from the skillet, add the cognac to the shrimp and let it ignite. When the flames die out, add the tomato-cream sauce and bring to a boil. Remove from the heat. Sprinkle the shrimp with the almonds and serve immediately. This goes well with steamed rice.

## shallots

These delicate small onions are especially good in wine sauces or subtly minced with herbs in cream sauces. Confess their aphrodisiac powers, and you may find your mate licking the bowl clean. Martial, the Roman poet and epigrammatist (A.D. 40–104), wrote

*If envious age relax the nuptial knot/Thy food be scallions and thy feast be shallot.*

# Lemon Grass Skewered
# Shrimp with Ginger

YIELD: 2 SERVINGS

1  pound/454g jumbo shrimp, peeled and deveined
2  lemon grass stalks or bamboo skewers,
   soaked in water for 4 hours or up to overnight
2  tablespoons olive oil
1  tablespoon fresh lemon juice
⅛  teaspoon freshly ground black pepper
½  teaspoon salt
1  teaspoon grated fresh ginger
1  tablespoon chopped fresh cilantro
1  tablespoon chopped fresh thyme

1. Spear the head end and tail of each shrimp with a lemon grass stalk, placing 5 shrimp on each stalk. In a medium nonreactive bowl, whisk the oil, lemon juice, pepper, salt, ginger, cilantro, and thyme. Place the shrimp skewers in a rectangular glass baking dish and pour the marinade over them. Cover with plastic wrap and let marinade in the refrigerator for at least 4 hours and no longer than 10 hours.

2. Heat a charcoal grill or broiler. Grill the shrimp until firm and pink, approximately 4 minutes. Serve on the skewers with roasted corn and grilled vegetables.

## ginger

Like many other foods that bring a tingling to the lips, mouth, and throat, ginger is esteemed in many cultures for its power of arousal. Never mind that it functions as a food preservative (even in the tropics) and wards off sea-sickness, the common cold, and bubonic plague; people love ginger for its erotic prop-erties. Turkish, Chinese, Arab, and Indian aphrodisiac recipes all call for ginger. The Senegalese chew ginger with kola nuts (containing caf-feine) for a truly stimulating rush. The English have per-fected the preservation of ginger in jam, candy, and syrup—a quick way to add a bit of risqué zest to a not-so-proper afternoon tea.

# Barbecued Shrimp
# with Sweet Potato Pancakes

Y I E L D :  2  S E R V I N G S

## Pancakes

½ pound/225g sweet potatoes, baked in a 350°F/
    180°C oven for approximately 50 minutes,
    then peeled
    Grated zest and juice of ½ orange
2 tablespoons packed light brown sugar, plus
    extra if needed

Pinch ground cloves
½ teaspoon ground cinnamon
    Pinch salt, plus extra if needed
½ cup/60g graham cracker crumbs
1 stick unsalted butter, clarified
    (see technique, page 14)

(see technique, page 14)

1. In a food processor, combine all the ingredients except graham cracker crumbs and butter. Process until blended. Season with additional salt and sugar if necessary.

2. Preheat the oven to 200°F/95°C and place a baking sheet in it. Form the sweet potato mixture into 4 patties. In a small bowl, combine the graham cracker crumbs and butter. Coat the patties with the graham cracker mixture. Heat a large skillet over medium-high heat. Add the pancakes and cook until golden on both sides. Transfer to the baking sheet in the oven to keep warm while preparing the shrimp.

## Barbecued Shrimp

1 teaspoon finely chopped garlic
¼ teaspoon finely chopped fresh rosemary
¼ teaspoon cracked black pepper
¼ teaspoon finely chopped fresh dill
¼ teaspoon grated lemon zest
¼ cup/60ml beer (any kind)
2 tablespoons seafood stock

1 teaspoon Worcestershire sauce
    Juice of 1 lemon
½ tablespoon unsalted butter
12 jumbo shrimp, peeled but tail left intact
    Sea salt to taste
2 tablespoons unsalted butter
2 deep-fried sprigs rosemary

1. In a small bowl, combine the garlic, chopped rosemary, black pepper, dill, and lemon zest. In a glass measuring cup combine the beer, seafood stock, Worcestershire sauce, and lemon juice.

2. In a large skillet, melt the butter over medium-high heat. Add the shrimp and the garlic-rosemary mixture. Season with sea salt. Cook, stirring, until the shrimp turn pink. (Be careful not to overcook the shrimp.) Remove the shrimp from the skillet and keep warm. Add the beer mixture and bring to a boil. Reduce the liquid slightly, add the shrimp, and remove the skillet from the heat. Swirl in the butter to create a saucelike consistency.

3. To serve, divide the pancakes between 2 warmed plates. Place 6 shrimp on each plate and spoon some sauce over them. Garnish with a deep-fried rosemary sprig.

## beer

No surprise here: The English and Irish fancy their native beers and ales as Cupid's beverage of choice before a good cuddle. You may find that lagers, pilsners, *bockbiers*, porters, and stouts from around the world complement the aphrodisiac foods found in this book—especially the spicy foods. With such a wide range of brews available, you will have flirty fun experimenting together.

# Baked Swordfish
# with Salmon Caviar Sauce

Yield: 2 servings

1  tablespoon vegetable oil
½  cup/70g peeled, seeded, and diced cucumber
¼  cup/60ml sour cream
1  teaspoon very finely chopped onion
1  teaspoon chopped fresh chives

½  pound/225g swordfish, cut into 1-inch-thick slices
    Salt and freshly ground black pepper to taste
2  tablespoons salmon caviar
2  sprigs thyme

1. Preheat the oven to 350°F/180°C. Lightly coat a baking sheet with the vegetable oil. In a small bowl, combine the cucumber, sour cream, onion, and chives; reserve.

2. Place the swordfish on the prepared baking sheet, season with salt and pepper, and bake for 7 minutes, or until opaque in the center. The swordfish may also be grilled, broiled, or sautéed with equally delicious results.

3. Transfer the swordfish to warmed plates. Add the salmon caviar to the cucumber sauce and drizzle the sauce around the fish. (Alternatively, serve the sauce in a sauceboat on the side.) Garnish each plate with a thyme sprig and serve immediately.

# Baked Red Mullet with Sun-Dried Tomato Tapenade

Yield: 2 servings

## Tapenade

4  ounces/120g sun-dried tomatoes packed in oil, drained (see sidebar)
4  ounces/120g kalamata olives, pitted
2  anchovy fillets
1  teaspoon capers, rinsed and drained
1  tablespoon chopped fresh cilantro
1  clove garlic
¼  cup/60ml olive oil
   Freshly ground black pepper to taste

In the bowl of a food processor, puree all the ingredients until smooth. Transfer to a container, cover, and chill in the refrigerator until ready to use.

## Red Mullet

2  ripe beefsteak tomatoes
1  slice white bread
5  tablespoons olive oil
½  clove garlic
   Two 7-ounce/200g fillets red mullet or red snapper
   Salt and freshly ground black pepper to taste
1  teaspoon chopped fresh thyme
¼  cup/60ml dry white wine
1  teaspoon chopped fresh parsley
5  fresh basil leaves, chopped

1. In a large saucepan, bring 2 quarts/2 liters water to a boil. Meanwhile, with a paring knife, cut out the stems from the tomatoes and make a small "X" in the opposite ends. Plunge into boiling water and boil until the skins are loosened, 10 to 20 seconds. With a slotted spoon, remove and place in a large bowl of cold water until cool enough to handle. Slip off the skins and cut the tomatoes in half. Gently but firmly squeeze the seeds; cut into medium dice and set aside.

2. Place the bread in the freezer for 30 minutes. Remove from the freezer and cut into ¼-inch/6mm dice. In a small skillet, heat 2 tablespoons olive oil over medium heat. Add the garlic and cook until browned but not burned, 2 to 3 minutes. Remove the garlic and discard.

3. Add the diced bread to the hot oil and sauté quickly, until nicely browned. Remove the croutons with a slotted spoon and drain on paper towels.

4. Preheat the oven to 350°F/180°C. Lightly coat a baking sheet with 2 tablespoons olive oil. Season the skin of the fish with salt and pepper. Sprinkle with the thyme. Place on the baking sheet, skin side up, and sprinkle with the wine. Bake for 8 to 10 minutes, or until opaque in the center.

5. Meanwhile, in a small skillet, heat the remaining 1 tablespoon olive oil over medium heat. Add the tomatoes and cook, stirring, for 3 minutes. Stir in the parsley and basil. Season with salt and pepper and remove from the heat.

6. To serve, remove the fish from the oven and spoon some tapenade down the center of each fillet. Place under the broiler for 3 to 4 minutes. Divide the fillets between 2 warmed plates. Spoon some sautéed tomatoes alongside each fillet, sprinkle with the croutons, and serve immediately.

# Calves' Liver with Leeks

Yield: 2 servings

1 beefsteak tomato
1 tablespoon all-purpose flour
　 Salt and freshly ground black pepper
　 Two 8-ounce/225g, ¼-inch/6mm-thick slices
　 calves' liver, membranes and veins removed
¼ cup/60ml vegetable oil
¼ cup/60ml dry white wine
¼ cup/60ml veal or beef stock

6 tablespoons/90g unsalted butter
1 cup/140g chopped leeks
1 clove garlic, crushed
¼ cup/60ml red wine vinegar
1 teaspoon maple syrup
1 teaspoon chopped fresh tarragon
1 teaspoon chopped fresh chives
1 teaspoon chopped fresh thyme

1. In a small saucepan, bring 1 quart/1 liter water to a boil. Meanwhile, with a paring knife, cut out the stem from the tomato and make a small "X" in the opposite end. Plunge the tomato in the boiling water and leave it in just until the skin is loosened, 10 to 20 seconds. With a slotted spoon, remove the tomato and rinse it under cold water until cool enough to handle. Slip off the skin and cut the tomato in half. Gently but firmly squeeze the seeds from the tomato halves. Cut into a medium dice and set aside.

2. Preheat the oven to 200°F/95°C. Place the flour in a shallow bowl. Season with salt and pepper. Lightly dredge the liver in the flour and shake off any excess coating.

3. In a skillet, heat the oil over high heat. Add the liver and sauté on each side very quickly until medium-rare in the middle, about 5 minutes. Transfer to a baking sheet, tent with aluminum foil and keep warm in the oven.

4. Pour any fat from the skillet and return it to medium heat. Add the wine and scrape up any browned bits from the bottom of the skillet. Bring to a simmer; reduce the wine by half. Add the stock and return to a simmer. Add 4 tablespoons/60g butter, a tablespoon at a time, whisking until thickened, being careful not to let the mixture overheat or the butter will separate. Stir in the reserved tomato. Keep warm over very low heat.

5. In a medium skillet, melt the remaining butter over medium-high heat. Add the leeks and garlic and cook, stirring, until the leeks are soft and transparent but not browned. Add the vinegar and bring to a simmer; reduce the liquid for 3 to 4 minutes. Add the maple syrup and chopped herbs. Season with salt and pepper.

6. To serve, spoon the leeks in the center of 2 plates. Top with the calves' liver. Spoon the sauce around the liver and serve immediately.

## liver

The ancient Greeks and Romans found this organ meat to arouse carnal desires. Horace, the first-century Roman poet and satirist, confirmed this when he described liver as a popular aphrodisiac in his day. Whereas Europeans favored calf liver, the Chinese preferred chicken liver to stimulate desire and raise endurance. The world regarded liver, high in iron and vitamins A and D, as an almost invincible cure-all until recently. Now, because of its high cholesterol content, we enjoy liver in moderation, just enough to profit from its other nutrients and restore our inner passions. Seek out some sensually smooth fatted goose liver (foie gras) for your next rendezvous. Nothing is so pleasurable as a rich foie gras gently sautéed or pressed into a pâté. Linger over each rich, creamy bite.

# Grilled Chicken Breast with Asparagus and Spicy Vinaigrette

These tiny seeds are pearls of sexual nutrition, acclaimed for their erotic effect since the era when Cleopatra, queen of Egypt (69–30 B.C.), seduced Julius Caesar and Marc Antony. Both the *Kama Sutra* and *The Perfumed Garden* include sesame concoctions, mixing the seeds with milk, flour, sugar, and other ingredients. Could Vatsayana and Nefzawí have known that sesame offers some of the finest plant protein available? With Middle Eastern sesame treats such as halvah and tahini now widely available in most supermarkets, exotic foreplay was never so tasty. Women find sesame especially enlivening.

### Spicy Vinaigrette

2 tablespoons corn oil
2 cloves garlic, sliced
¼ cup/40g finely cubed red and green bell pepper
1 tablespoon white wine vinegar
1 tablespoon fresh lime juice
½ teaspoon crushed red pepper

½ teaspoon cracked black pepper
½ teaspoon sesame seeds, toasted
½ teaspoon finely chopped fresh parsley
½ teaspoon grated fresh ginger
½ teaspoon chopped fresh chives
Pinch salt

1. In a skillet, heat the oil over medium heat. Add the garlic and cook, stirring, until it just begins to turn golden. Remove the skillet from the heat and set aside. Let cool. Remove the garlic from the oil and discard.

2. In a small nonreactive bowl, combine the remaining ingredients. Slowly whisk in the garlic-flavored oil. Reserve.

### Marinated Chicken

1 scallion, white and green parts, thinly sliced
½ tablespoon ancho chile powder
½ teaspoon dried oregano
½ teaspoon freshly ground black pepper

1 tablespoon chopped fresh cilantro
1 clove garlic, minced
1 tablespoon fresh lime juice
Two 6-ounce/180g boneless, skinless chicken breasts

In a medium nonreactive bowl, combine all the ingredients except the chicken. Stir to mix well. Add the chicken breasts and toss to coat. Cover with plastic wrap and let marinate in the refrigerator for 6 hours or up to overnight.

### To Assemble

18 spears asparagus
Salt to taste

2 tablespoons/30g butter
Cubed bell pepper and 2 whole red chiles for garnish

1. Heat a charcoal grill or broiler on medium heat. Meanwhile, bring a large saucepan of salted water to a boil. Prepare a large bowl of ice water. Pare down the base of any large asparagus spears with a vegetable peeler to remove the fibrous outer layer. Place the asparagus in the boiling water and cook until just tender but still bright green. Drain immediately and shock in the ice water to stop the cooking. Drain again and set aside.

2. Remove the chicken from the marinade and season with salt. Baste with the butter and grill lightly on both sides until well marked but still moist inside. (Alternatively, broil for 8 minutes.)

3. To serve, toss the asparagus with the vinaigrette and arrange on 2 plates with the grilled chicken breasts. Garnish the plates with the bell pepper and chiles.

# Oven-Roasted Quail Stuffed with Spinach and Goat Cheese

YIELD: 2 SERVINGS

## Spinach-Goat Cheese Filling

1 whole garlic head
1 teaspoon olive oil
  Salt and freshly ground black pepper to taste
1 teaspoon unsalted butter

½ small onion, finely diced
¼ cup washed and trimmed spinach leaves
1 ounce/30g fresh goat cheese
1 ounce/30g cooked ham, cut into ⅛-inch/3mm dice

1. Preheat the oven to 325°F/160°C. Pull the papery husks off the garlic head. Slice off the tip of the head to expose the cloves. Rub with the olive oil and season with salt and pepper. Place on a square of aluminum foil and sprinkle with a bit of water. Pinch the edges of the foil together and place on a baking sheet. Roast for 30 to 45 minutes, or until very tender. Let cool. Squeeze the garlic pulp from the skins into a small bowl. Set aside.

2. In a medium skillet, melt the butter over medium heat. Add the onion and roasted garlic and cook, stirring, until golden, about 5 minutes. Add the spinach and cook, stirring, until the leaves wilt. Add the goat cheese and ham and stir to incorporate. Remove from the heat and let cool. Transfer to a small bowl, cover, and chill until needed.

## Risotto

2 ½ cups/625ml chicken or mushroom stock
2 tablespoons olive oil
2 tablespoons/30g unsalted butter
¼ cup diced onion
¼ cup/30g diced shiitake mushroom caps

½ cup/100g Arborio rice
1 tablespoon snipped fresh chives
¼ cup/25g finely grated Parmesan cheese
  Salt and freshly ground black pepper to taste

1. In a medium saucepan, bring the stock to a boil. Reduce the heat and hold at a simmer.

2. Meanwhile, in a medium cast-iron skillet, heat the olive oil and 1 tablespoon/15g butter over medium heat. Add the onion and mushrooms and cook, stirring, until the onion is softened, about 5 minutes. Add the rice and stir with a wooden spoon until well coated, about 4 minutes.

3. Slowly add enough stock to cover the rice, about ½ cup/125ml. Simmer, stirring continuously, until the liquid is almost absorbed. Add another ½ cup of stock and cook, stirring, until almost absorbed. Continue to add stock, ½ cup at a time, until the risotto has cooked for a total of 15 minutes and is creamy but still slightly firm in the center.

4. Add the chives, the remaining 1 tablespoon butter, and the Parmesan. Cook, stirring, for 1 to 2 minutes more. Season with salt and pepper. Set aside and keep warm on the stove.

## marjoram

One of those herbs that can go either way, marjoram may either stimulate or quell desire. Folklore aside, I lean toward the belief that marjoram works as an aphrodisiac when added to stews and tomato, egg, or cheese dishes. And if it causes women to have lewd dreams, as one archival treatise testifies, so much the better.

*continued on page 100*

### Vegetables

1 cup/140g triangular carrot chunks
1 cup/140g triangular parsnip chunks
½ cup/60g pearl onions

2 tablespoons olive oil
Salt to taste

Preheat the oven to 350°F/180°C. In a small roasting pan, combine the carrots, parsnips, and pearl onions. Drizzle with the oil and toss to coat. Season with salt. Roast in the oven for 20 minutes, or until the vegetables are tender. Remove from the oven and reserve. Keep warm.

### Quail

2 quail, boned but with wing and leg bones left intact
Salt and freshly ground black pepper to taste
½ large leek, light green part only

2 sprigs each marjoram, thyme, and rosemary
2 celery leaves

1. Preheat the oven to 400°F/200°C. Spread the quail out on a work surface and season with salt and pepper. Divide the filling between the quail, spooning it into the cavity. Close the quail and tie them shut with kitchen string. Roast in the oven for 20 minutes, until just cooked.

2. Meanwhile, bring a small saucepan of salted water to a boil. Place the leek in the boiling water and cook until just tender but still bright green. Drain immediately and cut into julienne strips.

3. To serve, spoon some risotto in each of 2 soup plates. Remove the string from the quail and place a quail on each risotto mound. Spoon some roasted vegetables alongside and garnish with the herb sprigs, celery leaves, and leek. Serve immediately.

# Crispy Ginger Duck with Poached Pears

Y I E L D : 2 S E R V I N G S

### Duck

1 Muscovy duck (about 3 pounds/1.4kg)
Salt and coarsely ground black pepper to taste

One 3-inch/7.5cm slice fresh ginger, peeled
1 tablespoon canola oil

1. Preheat the oven to 450°F/230°C. Season the cavity of the duck with salt and pepper. Place the slice of ginger in the cavity and season the outside of the duck with salt and pepper.

2. In a large skillet, heat the oil over high heat. Sear the duck on all sides until browned. Transfer the duck to a large roasting pan and roast for 50 minutes. Remove from the oven, tent with aluminum foil, and keep warm.

*continued on page 102*

## Cabbage Garnish

2  tablespoons/30g unsalted butter or duck fat
¼  head Savoy cabbage, shredded
¼  pound/120g shiitake mushrooms (about 12 large
    ones), stemmed and sliced
1  teaspoon sugar
    Salt and freshly ground black pepper to taste

Pour off the fat from the skillet used to sear the ducks and add the butter (or duck fat) to the skillet. Melt the butter (or duck fat) over medium-high heat. Add the cabbage, mushrooms, and sugar. Cook, stirring, until the cabbage is softened. Season with salt and pepper. Set aside and keep warm.

## Sauce

1  duck bone
1  cup/140g chopped shallots
3  tablespoons tomato paste
1  cup/250ml dry red wine

¼  cup/60ml brandy
¼  cup/60ml port wine
¼  cup/60ml veal stock
    Salt and freshly ground black pepper to taste

In a medium saucepan, roast the duck bone and shallots about 4 minutes on high heat. Add the tomato paste and roast until browned; add the red wine and brandy and bring to a boil. Reduce the heat and simmer until the liquid is reduced by 90 percent. Add the port and stock and reduce until the sauce coats the back of a spoon. Strain through a fine sieve into a small saucepan. Season with salt and pepper. Reserve and keep warm.

## Poached Pears

1  cup/250ml dry red wine
    Grated zest of 2 oranges
    Grated zest of ½ lemon
1  cinnamon stick

2  tablespoons sugar
2  ripe pears
    Thyme sprigs for garnish

1. In a small nonreactive saucepan, combine the wine, orange zest, lemon zest, cinnamon stick, and sugar. Bring to a boil. Add the pears. Reduce the heat and simmer the pears for 15 minutes. Remove from the heat.

2. Cut a wedge out of each pear and slice thinly into a fan. Leave the pears in their poaching liquid until ready to serve.

## To Assemble

1. Remove the breast from the duck and slice it on the diagonal.

2. To serve, spoon a pile of cabbage garnish in the center of each of 2 plates. Fan out the breast meat slices and pear slices over the cabbage at the bottom of the plates. Arrange a duck leg and remaining pear at the top of each plate. Spoon the sauce around the duck, garnish with thyme, and serve immediately.

# cabbage

There is a reason why French lovers affectionately address each other as "my little cabbage" (*mon petit chou*). This cruciferous vegetable has provided us with fiber and vitamin C for nearly 4,000 years, and its libido-lifting effect was noted by Apicius, the first-century Roman cookbook author. In fact, the Romans dedicated their young cabbages to Priapus, their god of fertility and viniculture. You may benefit by chopping a few leaves into your next salad. Try the red ones—they add tantalizing color. And remember the *real* reason babies are harvested from under cabbage leaves.

# Grilled Rib-Eye Steak with Caramelized Onions and Onion Rings

YIELD: 2 SERVINGS

5 tablespoons/75g unsalted butter
1 pound/454g red onions, sliced
2 tablespoons sugar
2 tablespoons balsamic vinegar
⅔ cup/150ml dry white wine
1 tablespoon chopped fresh thyme
2 cloves garlic, minced
   Salt and freshly ground black pepper to taste

4 cups/1l peanut oil or light olive oil
½ cup/60g all-purpose flour
2 teaspoons paprika
1 large Spanish onion, thinly sliced and separated into rings
2 medium carrots, cut into ¼-inch/6mm-thick sticks
12 haricots verts or string beans
2 rib-eye steaks, 7 to 10 ounces/200 to 290g each
1 tablespoon/15g unsalted butter

1. To make the carmelized onions, melt the butter over medium heat in a medium nonreactive skillet. Add the onions and cook, stirring, until lightly browned, 15 to 20 minutes. Add the sugar and cook, stirring, until caramelized. Add the vinegar and cook until evaporated. Add the wine, thyme, and garlic. Reduce the heat to low and cook, stirring occasionally, for another 10 minutes. Season with salt and pepper. Remove from the heat and reserve.

2. Make the onion rings: in a deep heavy saucepan, heat the oil to 350°F/180°C. (A small piece of bread dropped into the oil should float to the surface almost immediately and brown within 45 seconds.)

3. Meanwhile, in a shallow bowl, combine the flour and paprika. Season with salt and pepper. Lightly dredge the onion rings in the flour and toss them in a mesh strainer to shake off any excess coating. Deep-fry in batches until golden brown, about 2 minutes. Drain on paper towels and keep warm.

4. Preheat a charcoal grill, if using. Meanwhile, bring a large saucepan of salted water to a boil. Prepare a large bowl of ice water. Add the carrots to the boiling water and cook until tender, about 4 minutes. Remove the carrots with a strainer and plunge them into the ice water to stop the cooking. Repeat the procedure with the *haricots verts* and drain.

5. Season the steaks with salt and pepper. Grill on both sides to the desired doneness. (Alternatively, pan-fry the steaks in a skillet.) In a skillet, melt the butter over medium heat. Add the carrots and *haricots verts* and cook until heated through. Season with salt and pepper.

6. To serve, arrange a steak at the bottom of 2 plates. At the top of the plates arrange the confit and onion rings and surround with the sautéed vegetables. Serve immediately.

## beef

European doctors have touted beef as a fortifying and strengthening food since the Renaissance. Dr. Nicolas Venette recommended beef marrow in his 1686 book, *Tableau de l'Amour Conjugal*—a guide for newlyweds so popular it was reprinted in 1814, over 100 years later. European chefs understood this as well, creating beef dishes to satisfy the passions of hungry kings and nobles. Dishes like Châteaubriand gastronome (a thick steak studded with diced truffles and served with cooked chestnuts), tournedos Rossini (a pan-fried steak on a bed of artichoke bottoms, topped with truffle slices and a fried goose liver), and osso buco (baked beef marrow with tomatoes and onions) incorporated many aphrodisiac foods and were truly the stuff of highbrow fantasy. And as it turns out, beef packs a hefty protein punch, as well as vitamin B12, iron, and zinc—none of which can hurt your sex life.
When grilling up a fantasy of your own for that special someone, take care to choose the best grade of beef you can—go for prime or choice—and always handle it with clean hands and immaculate utensils. Then dim the lights and listen for that sizzle.

# Pepper Steak

YIELD: 2 SERVINGS

Two 8-ounce/225g sirloin steaks or
filets mignons
½ cup/80g mixed peppercorns
(green, red, black, and white)
2 tablespoons Dijon mustard
Salt to taste
4 tablespoons/60g butter

1 onion, finely chopped
¼ cup/60ml cognac
Dash of red wine
¼ cup/60ml demi-glace
¼ cup/60ml heavy cream
1 tablespoon Tabasco sauce
Thyme sprigs for garnish

1. Wipe the steaks clean with a damp cloth. Coarsely crush the white peppercorns only using a mortar and pestle, or place them in a cloth and crush with a rolling pin. Combine with the other peppercorns on a plate. Rub the steaks with mustard and salt. Then press the steaks firmly on both sides into the peppercorns. Reserve any peppercorns that were not picked up by the steaks. Cover the steaks with plastic wrap and let marinate for 30 minutes.

2. Preheat the oven to 180°F/80°C. In a large skillet, heat 3 tablespoons/45g of the butter. Add the steaks and brown briefly over medium heat, 3 minutes per side. Remove the steaks and keep warm in the oven.

3. In the same skillet, melt the remaining butter. Add the onion and cook until wilted. Deglaze the pan with the cognac and wine. Reduce by half. Add the demi-glace, stirring continously with a whisk. Add the cream and cook to reduce and thicken the sauce. Add the reserved peppercorns to the sauce and simmer for 1 minute. Add the Tabasco sauce and taste and correct the seasoning.

4. Place the pepper steaks on plates, surround with sauce, and garnish with thyme.

## peppercorns

These spicy berries grow on the *Piper nigrum* vine, native to India or Malaysia. They are green when picked, then turn red, yellow, brown, and finally black as they dry in the sun. White peppercorns are simply fully ripe black peppercorns stripped of their dark husk. Both the *Kama Sutra* and *The Perfumed Garden* make mention of pepper, which flavors and preserves food and creates excitement by increasing the flow of saliva. Europeans also knew of pepper's value and went to great lengths to obtain it, as well as other spices, from the East. For the richest, sexiest aroma, grind or crush your peppercorns as needed just before using.

# Surf and Turf in a Béarnaise Sauce

YIELD: 2 SERVINGS

## Surf and Turf

Two 5-ounce/150g lobster tails in their shells
2 tablespoons fresh lemon juice
4 tablespoons/60g butter, melted

Salt and freshly ground black pepper to taste
Two 5-ounce/150g filet mignon steaks
1 tablespoon olive oil

1. Preheat the oven to 375°F/190°C. Slice the lobster tails open; remove the tail shells and reserve. Sprinkle the lobster meat with lemon juice, glaze with the melted butter, and season with salt and pepper. Place the lobster meat and shells on a baking sheet and roast for 5 to 6 minutes, or until the lobster is well-done but not overcooked.

2. Preheat the broiler. Brush the steaks with the olive oil and season with salt and pepper. Broil under high heat for 3 minutes on each side.

## Béarnaise Sauce

1 tablespoon chopped shallot
3 cracked black peppercorns
1 tablespoon dried tarragon
3 tablespoons tarragon vinegar
4 tablespoons white vinegar
5 tablespoons water

3 egg yolks
¾ cup/200ml clarified butter, warmed (see technique, page 14)
1 teaspoon coarsely chopped fresh tarragon
1 teaspoon coarsely chopped fresh chervil
Salt and freshly ground black pepper to taste

1. In a skillet over medium heat, combine the shallot, peppercorns, tarragon, tarragon vinegar, and white vinegar. Bring to a boil and reduce by half. Add the water to the reduction; remove from the heat and let cool.

2. Combine the egg yolks and the reduction in a stainless steel bowl or the top of a double boiler. Set over simmering water and whip the yolk mixture until it forms ribbons and triples in volume. (The mixture should be light, firm, and creamy.) Add the clarified butter gradually, whipping constantly. Strain to remove any cooked egg particles if necessary.

3. Add the chopped herbs and season with salt and pepper. Be careful not to overcook the sauce; it should be warm but not hot.

4. To serve, place the cooked lobster tails and steaks on 2 plates. Garnish each plate with a lobster shell and spoon the sauce on the steak and lobster. This dish goes well with assorted vegetables and potatoes.

# Rack of Lamb with Roasted Garlic Mashed Potatoes

Yield: 2 servings

## Roasted Garlic Mashed Potatoes

1 whole head garlic
1 teaspoon plus ¼ cup/60ml olive oil
Salt and freshly ground black pepper to taste
4 medium red potatoes, peeled

2 tablespoons chopped fresh basil
¼ cup/60ml heavy cream, warmed, plus extra if needed
2 tablespoons/30g unsalted butter
2 ounces/60g Parmesan cheese, freshly grated

1. Preheat the oven to 325°F/160°C. Pull the papery husks off the garlic head. Slice off the tip of the head to expose the cloves. Rub with 1 teaspoon olive oil and season with salt and pepper. Place on a square of aluminum foil and sprinkle with a bit of water. Pinch the edges of the foil together and place on a baking sheet. Roast for 30 to 45 minutes, or until very tender. Let cool. Squeeze garlic pulp from skins into a small bowl. Set aside.

2. Bring a large saucepan of salted water to a boil. Add the potatoes and cook until soft. Drain and place in a large mixing bowl with the garlic puree, the remaining ¼ cup/60ml oil, and the basil, cream, and butter. Using an electric mixture or large balloon whisk, beat the potatoes until very smooth. If the potatoes are a bit too dry, add more cream. Whisk in the cheese. Season with salt and pepper. Transfer to the top of a double boiler; cover and keep warm.

## Lamb and Crust

2 tablespoons vegetable oil
1 rack of lamb with 8 chops, frenched
Salt and freshly ground black pepper to taste
2 tablespoons Dijon mustard

½ cup/60g fresh bread crumbs or finely cut white bread
½ cup/15g finely chopped fresh herbs, such as basil, parsley, thyme, and chervil
4 tablespoons/60g unsalted butter, melted
2 sprigs rosemary

1. Preheat the oven to 450°F/230°C. In a large skillet, heat the oil over high heat. Season the rack of lamb with salt and pepper and add it to the pan. Sear on all sides until well browned. Let cool.

2. Brush the lamb with the mustard. Prepare the herb crust: Mix the bread crumbs very well with the herbs and melted butter. Gently press this mixture on top of the rack of lamb. Transfer the lamb to a roasting pan and roast for 12 to 16 minutes, until medium-rare in the center. Remove from the oven, tent with aluminum foil, and let rest for 5 minutes. Reserve the pan juices for garnish.

3. To serve, slice the lamb between every other bone and serve 2 chops on each plate. Accompany with garlic mashed potatoes and garnish with a sprig of rosemary and the reserved pan juices.

## lamb

The lamb or young sheep was a pagan symbol for bounty, an Old Testament symbol of the Israelites, and a New Testament symbol of peace and innocence. And through the ages lamb has held the status of potent aphrodisiac, thanks to its uniquely succulent, tender meat. Its sensual appeal is no secret to those of the Middle East, Greece, and North Africa, who combine it with other Mediterranean aphrodisiacs, including rosemary, garlic, mint, eggplant, and white beans. The English dress their lamb with mint sauce, while diners here reach for mint jelly. Lamb is high in protein, B vitamins, iron, and zinc and offers a more complex flavor than beef. You'll also notice that it's less marbled than beef and that you can easily remove the outer layer of fat. No entree says "special occasion" quite like a beautifully presented rack of lamb. Or if you and your lover indulge in roast leg, crown roast, shoulder, chops, or shanks, make it into a lavish pagan ritual and create your own eternal spring.

# Lamb Chops with Mint-Cilantro Chutney and Indian Potato Pancakes

Yield: 2 servings

### Marinated Lamb

1 ½ cups/375ml plain yogurt
Juice of 3 limes
1 ½ tablespoons ground coriander
1 tablespoon ground ginger
¾ teaspoon cayenne pepper

¾ teaspoon ground cinnamon
¾ teaspoon ground cardamom
¾ teaspoon ground cloves
½ teaspoon freshly ground black pepper
8 lamb chops, frenched

In a large bowl, combine all the ingredients except the lamb chops. Stir to mix well. Add the lamb and toss to coat. Cover with plastic wrap and let marinate in the refrigerator overnight.

### Mint-Cilantro Chutney

¼ cup/6g fresh cilantro leaves
3 tablespoons fresh mint leaves
1 teaspoon finely chopped fresh ginger
½ teaspoon finely chopped garlic

½ serrano chile, seeded and chopped
Grated zest and juice of 1 lemon
¼ teaspoon salt
1 cup/250ml peanut oil

In a food processor, combine all the ingredients except the oil. Process until smooth. With the motor running, slowly add the oil in a steady stream. Transfer the chutney to a small bowl and cover with plastic wrap. Set aside.

### Lamb Jus

1 teaspoon olive oil
1 teaspoon red curry paste

1 cup/250ml lamb stock

In a medium saucepan, heat the oil over medium heat. Add the curry paste and cook, stirring, until fragrant. Add the stock and bring to a boil. Reduce the heat to low and simmer, stirring occasionally, until reduced by three-fourths. Keep warm until ready to serve.

## Indian Potato Pancakes

*1 pound/454g russet potatoes, preferable Idaho, peeled*
*1 tablespoon peanut oil*
*1 tablespoon mustard seeds*
*3 tablespoons/45g unsalted butter, clarified*
*   (see technique, page 14)*
*½ tablespoon ground cumin*
*1 medium onion, chopped*

*1 tablespoon finely chopped garlic*
*2 tablespoons crushed curry leaves*
*1 teaspoon turmeric*
*2 tablespoons chopped fresh cilantro*
*1 teaspoon salt*
*1 serrano chile, finely chopped*
*1 teaspoon freshly ground black pepper*

1. In a food processor with a medium disk, grate the potatoes. Place the potatoes in a bowl of ice water. Set aside.

2. In a skillet, heat ½ tablespoon oil over medium-high heat. Add the mustard seeds and stir until they begin to pop. Immediately transfer the seeds to a large bowl. Add the clarified butter, cumin, onion, garlic, curry leaves, and turmeric to the mustard seeds. Stir to mix well.

3. Preheat the oven to 200°F/95°C and place a baking sheet in it. Drain the potatoes, dry them well, and add to the bowl of spices. Toss carefully to mix well but be sure not to break the potato pieces. Add the cilantro, salt, chile, and black pepper. Mold the potato mixture into 4 pancakes.

4. In a large skillet, heat the remaining ½ table-spoon oil over medium-high heat. Sauté the pancakes until golden on both sides. Transfer to the baking sheet in the oven to keep warm while cooking the lamb.

## To Assemble

*1 teaspoon salt*

*½ tablespoon unsalted butter*

1. Heat a charcoal grill. Remove the lamb from the marinade and season with salt on all sides. Grill lightly on both sides. (Alternatively, pan-fry the chops in a hot skillet.) With a whisk, swirl the butter into the lamb jus.

2. To serve, place 2 potato pancakes on each of 2 warmed plates. Place 2 lamb chops alongside each pancake. Spoon the mint-cilantro chutney around the lamb and the lamb jus around the pancakes. Serve immediately.

# coriander

Europeans have utilized the aromatic seeds of this herb in love potions since the Middle Ages. Coriander finds its way into dishes ranging from apple pie to Indian curries and is also widely featured in Chinese and Latin American cooking. The leaves, known as cilantro, are currently all the rage in chic big-city restaurants. And if you thought that was just another culinary trend, well, now you know the *real* reason.

# Roasted Pheasant Breast with Savoy Cabbage, Garlic Cloves, and Sage

YIELD: 2 SERVINGS

## sage

This herb's velvety leaves may inspire even the most practical person to divulge a softer, more romantic side. Contemporary Italians steep sage in water or red wine for a feeling of friskiness. Better yet, you might try sage with hare, poultry dressing, or a morning-after omelet.

### Cabbage

2  ounces/60g bacon, finely chopped
1  small head Savoy cabbage, shredded
2  tablespoons/30g unsalted butter

¾  cup/200ml dry white wine
   Chopped fresh oregano to taste
   Salt and freshly ground black pepper to taste

In a skillet over medium-low heat, cook the bacon until the fat is reduced, then add the cabbage, butter, and wine. Cover the pan and braise the mixture until the cabbage is tender, about 8 minutes. Remove from the heat and season with the oregano, salt, and pepper. Keep warm on the stove.

### Pheasant

2  pheasant breasts (about 1 pound/454g)
   Salt and freshly ground black pepper to taste
1  teaspoon chopped fresh thyme, plus 2 sprigs
   for garnish
2  tablespoons olive oil
1  tablespoon/15g unsalted butter

12  pearl onions
 8  cloves garlic, unpeeled, boiled in water for
    3 minutes and drained
 1  bunch fresh sage
½  cup/125ml chicken stock

1. Preheat the oven to 450°F/230°C. Season the breasts with salt, pepper, and thyme. In a large, heavy, ovenproof cast-iron skillet, heat the olive oil and butter over medium-high heat. Add the breasts, skin side up, and sauté until golden, about 2 minutes. Turn them so they are skin side down.

2. Add the pearl onions, garlic cloves, and sage (set aside a few sprigs for garnish) to the pan and transfer to the oven. Roast for 5 minutes, or until almost cooked. Remove from the oven and place over medium heat. Pour enough stock into the skillet to come halfway up the sides of the pheasant breasts and bring to a simmer. When the breasts are fully cooked but still moist, transfer them to a platter and tent with aluminum foil to keep warm. There should still be liquid in the skillet.

3. Simmer the remaining stock until the onions are tender. Season with salt and pepper.

4. To serve, slice the pheasant on the diagonal and fan the slices over a mound of cabbage at the bottom of 2 plates. Arrange the onions and garlic along the top of the plates and spoon the sauce around the plate. Garnish with the reserved sage and thyme and serve immediately.

# Grilled Venison Steak with Cranberry Sauce and Celeriac

YIELD: 2 SERVINGS

## venison

Deer meat has a masculine charisma and appeals to the hunter in every man—even if it is ranch raised, federally inspected, and professionally butchered. The variables associated with wild venison include toughness due to age, strong flavor due to the deer's diet of pine needles and juniper berries, and the dangers of inexperienced handling. You and your partner will warm up to its mild, gamy flavor complemented by hearty vegetable aphrodisiacs like cabbage and mushrooms. It contains less fat than beef and offers plenty of protein, iron, phosphorus, B vitamins, and potassium to keep the evening interesting.

A couple of venison steaks shared by a crackling fire may evoke the fantasy of an enchanted forest outside and inspire you to kick off your buckskin slippers and stray from the trodden trail.

### Pureed Celeriac

½  knob celeriac, peeled and sliced
Juice of ½ lemon

1  tablespoon/15g unsalted butter
Salt and freshly ground white pepper to taste

Bring a large saucepan of salted water to a boil. Add the celeriac and lemon juice and cook until soft, 20 to 25 minutes. Drain and transfer to to a food processor. Puree until smooth. Add the butter and season with salt and pepper. Puree again until combined. Transfer to the top of a double boiler set over simmering (not boiling) water; cover and keep warm.

### Fried Celeriac

1  knob celeriac, peeled and julienned

1  cup/250ml oil

Rinse the celeriac in cold water and dry thoroughly. Heat the oil in a cast-iron skillet to 325°F/160°C and add the celeriac. Fry for 2 minutes. Drain well and transfer to a baking sheet lined with absorbent paper. When ready to use, finish the celeriac in a 375°F oven until golden brown and cooked through. Drain well again.

### Cranberry Sauce

4  tablespoons/60g unsalted butter
1  tablespoon minced shallot
1  clove garlic, minced
1  cup/100g cranberries
2  tablespoons sugar

½  cup/125ml dry red wine
1 ¼  cups/310ml reduced venison or beef stock
1  teaspoon chopped fresh sage
Salt and freshly ground black pepper to taste

1. In a large skillet, melt 1 tablespoon butter/15g over medium heat. Add the shallot and garlic and cook, stirring, until soft. Add the cranberries and sugar and stir until combined.

2. Add the wine. Maintaining medium heat, bring to a simmer and reduce the liquid by three-fourths. Add the stock and sage and reduce by one-third. Strain through a fine sieve into a clean saucepan and bring to a boil. Whisk in the remaining 3 tablespoons/45g butter and remove from the heat. Season with salt and pepper and keep warm.

### Sautéed Mushrooms

2   *tablespoons/30g unsalted butter or vegetable oil*
1   *clove garlic, minced*
1   *tablespoon finely chopped shallot*

6   *ounces/180g mixed fresh mushrooms*
    *(chanterelles, shiitakes, or porcini), quartered if large*
1   *teaspoon finely chopped fresh parsley*

In a large skillet, melt the butter over medium heat. Add the garlic, shallot, and mushrooms and sauté until tender, about 3 minutes. Sprinkle with the parsley and set aside.

### Venison

*Two 6-ounce/180g venison loin steaks*
1   *tablespoon olive oil*
1   *tablespoon crushed juniper berries*

*Salt and freshly ground black pepper to taste*
2   *tablespoons cranberries*
    *Chopped fresh parsley for garnish*

1. Heat a charcoal grill. Lightly coat both sides of the venison steaks with the oil. Season with the juniper berries, salt, and pepper and grill until rare, about 5 minutes per side.

2. To serve, coat 2 plates with the celeriac puree. Begin slicing the venison steaks and place on the puree. Place the fried celeriac behind each partially sliced steak, on the top of the plate. Surround each plate with sautéed mushrooms and cranberry sauce. Garnish the plate with the cranberries and parsley.

# Tenderloin Tips Stroganoff

YIELD: 2 SERVINGS

4   *tablespoons/60g unsalted butter*
    *One 12-ounce/345g beef fillet, cut into*
    *½-by-¼-inch/12-by-6mm strips*
1   *medium onion, cut into strips*
8   *ounces/225g mushrooms, sliced*
⅓   *cup/75ml cognac*

1   *cup/250ml heavy cream*
    *Salt and freshly ground black pepper to taste*
2   *kosher pickles, cut into strips*
1   *small red beet, cooked and cut into strips*
2   *tablespoons sour cream*

1. In a large skillet, melt 3 tablespoons/45g butter over medium-high heat. Add the fillet strips and sauté briefly on all sides until browned. Transfer to a strainer placed over a bowl and allow the beef to drain. Reserve the beef and its juices separately.

2. In the same skillet, melt the remaining 1 tablespoon/15g butter over medium-high heat. Add the onion and mushrooms and cook, stirring, until the onion is wilted. Add the cognac and scrape up any browned bits from the bottom of the skillet. Add the reserved meat juices and cream and cook, stirring, until the sauce is reduced and thickened, 10 to 15 minutes. Season with salt and pepper. Add the reserved beef strips to the sauce and heat through.

3. To serve, transfer the stroganoff to a warmed platter and garnish with the pickles, beet, and sour cream.

## juniper

This purplish blue berry is the fruit of a hardy evergreen shrub that can withstand the coldest winters. The Dutch invented gin, a distilled spirit from juniper, which caught on in England in the 1700s. The English applauded gin's fair price and the herbal zing juniper lent their love lives. They also mixed the berry into aphrodisiac potions. No need to search through dusty volumes for those concoctions of old, however, for game, salmon, or cheese garnished with a bit of juniper will warm the heart of even the most frigid partner. And a thimbleful of gin has been known to warm the spirit as well.

# sweet

*Sweet temptations—the title of this chapter says it all.  End your aphrodisiac meal on a memorable note.*

# temptations

*Get creative with these desserts. Feed them to your lover with a spoon—or with your fingers.*

# Crème Brûlée

2 cups/500ml heavy cream
½ vanilla bean, split
¼ cup/60g plus 1 tablespoon sugar

4 large egg yolks
4 tablespoons packed light brown sugar

1. Preheat the oven to 250°F/120°C. In a medium saucepan, slowly bring the cream to a boil over medium-low heat. Reduce the heat to low. Use the tip of a blunt knife to scrape the vanilla bean seeds into the cream. Gently simmer, stirring occasionally, until the vanilla has infused the cream, about 15 minutes.

2. In a mixing bowl, whisk the sugar and egg yolks until lightly colored. Strain the vanilla-infused cream through a medium sieve into the egg yolk mixture. Whisk until well blended.

3. Bring a large kettle of water to a boil. Line a small roasting pan with a folded kitchen towel. Place four 4-ounce/120g soufflé dishes or ramekins in the roasting pan. Ladle the cream mixture into the ramekins. Pour enough boiling water into the roasting pan to come halfway up the sides of the dishes. Bake for 1 hour, or until lightly set. Transfer the ramekins to a wire rack and let cool. Cover with plastic wrap and chill in the refrigerator.

4. Place the brown sugar in a medium sieve and sprinkle it over the custards. Place the soufflé dishes or ramekins under the broiler for about 1 minute, or until the sugar has caramelized. Serve immediately.

# Chocolate Soufflé

1 cup/250ml whole milk

2 ounces/60g unsweetened cocoa powder

3 ½ ounces/100g semisweet chocolate, chopped

2 ounces/60g bittersweet (not unsweetened) chocolate, chopped

2 cups/500ml egg whites

1 ounce/30g powdered egg whites

Juice of ½ lemon

½ cup/120g sugar

¼ cup/60ml light corn syrup

2 ½ tablespoons water

2 tablespoons confectioners' sugar

1. Preheat the oven to 400°F/200°C. Lightly butter two 8-ounce/225g soufflé dishes or ramekins. Dust the molds with sugar; tilt to coat and tap out the excess.

2. In a medium heavy saucepan, bring the milk to a boil. As soon as it boils, remove it from the heat and add the cocoa powder and chopped chocolate. Whisk until the mixture is smooth and no small lumps of chocolate remain. Return the saucepan to the stove and place it over medium-high heat. Bring the mixture to a boil and then remove it from the heat. Set aside.

3. Place the fresh egg whites, powdered egg whites, and lemon juice in a clean, grease-free mixing bowl. With an electric mixer, beat on low speed until frothy.

4. In a small heavy saucepan, combine the sugar, the corn syrup, and the water over medium heat. Bring to a boil and cook without stirring until a candy thermometer registers 250°F/120°C (soft-ball stage). Immediately remove from the heat and very slowly pour into the egg whites, beating continuously on medium-high speed, making sure to avoid pouring the syrup on the beaters. Continue beating until the bottom of the mixing bowl is warm—but not hot—to the touch, about 5 minutes.

5. Transfer the chocolate mixture to a large bowl. (If it has dried out slightly, thin with a small amount of water or rum.) With a rubber spatula, fold one-quarter of the whipped egg whites into the chocolate mixture. Add the remaining whites and fold in carefully, taking care not to deflate them.

6. Using a pastry bag with a 1 ½-inch/4cm opening, pipe the mixture into the prepared molds to the rim of the molds. Alternatively, you may use a resealable bag clipped at one corner. (The molded soufflés will keep at room temperature for several hours before baking or in the refrigerator for up to 12 hours. If refrigerated, let stand at room temperature for about 1 hour before baking.)

7. Place the soufflé molds on a baking sheet and bake for 10 minutes, or until doubled in height and golden. Place the confectioners' sugar in a sieve and sprinkle it over the tops of the soufflés. Serve immediately.

# Chocolate Mousse

4 ½ ounces/130g semisweet chocolate, chopped
⅓ cup/75g unsalted butter
2 large egg yolks
3 large egg whites

1 tablespoon sugar
Strawberry sauce (page 133), chocolate sauce
(page 154), and Lady Fingers (page 161)

1. Place the chocolate in the top of a double boiler set over 1 inch/2.5cm of simmering (not boiling) water. Whisk until the chocolate is smooth and no small lumps remain. Remove the pan from the heat and stir in the butter. Let cool completely. Add the egg yolks, one by one, stirring well after each addition. Set aside.

2. Place the egg whites in a clean, grease-free mixing bowl. With an electric mixer, beat on low speed until frothy. Increase the speed to medium and gradually add the sugar. When the sugar is incorporated, increase the speed to medium-high and beat until the whites hold stiff but not dry peaks.

3. With a rubber spatula, fold the reserved chocolate mixture into the egg whites until well combined. Refrigerate until firm. Spoon onto a chilled dessert plate with a large spoon, and garnish with the strawberry sauce, chocolate sauce, and lady fingers. Alternatively, you may divide the mousse among 4 glass bowls, cover with plastic wrap, and chill until firm. Garnish each bowl with strawberry sauce, a strawberry half, and a mint sprig.

# Flourless Chocolate Cake with Fresh Fruit

YIELD: 10 SERVINGS

1 pound/454g semisweet chocolate, broken into pieces
1 tablespoon pure vanilla extract
1 tablespoon dark rum
¾ cup/200ml strong brewed coffee
8 large eggs

½ cup/120g sugar
¾ cup/200ml heavy cream
  Whipped cream, assorted fresh fruit, and mint
  leaves for garnish

1. Preheat the oven to 300°F/150°C. Butter a 12-inch/30cm terrine mold and refrigerate it until ready to use. Chill a large mixing bowl.

2. Place the chocolate, vanilla, rum, and coffee in the top of a double boiler set over 1 inch/2.5cm of simmering (not boiling) water. Whisk until the chocolate is smooth and no small lumps remain. Turn off the heat and remove the chocolate from the hot water. Transfer the mixture to a large bowl.

3. In a medium mixing bowl, combine the eggs and sugar. With an electric mixer, beat until pale in color, stopping 2 or 3 times to scrape down the sides of the bowl. Add some of the chocolate mixture and beat until incorporated. Pour this mixture into the remaining chocolate mixture. Stir until combined.

4. Bring a large kettle of water to a boil. In the chilled mixing bowl, whip the cream until soft peaks form. With a rubber spatula, fold the whipped cream into the chocolate mixture until just combined. Pour the mixture into the prepared terrine mold and cover with aluminum foil. Place in a roasting pan and pour enough boiling water into the pan to come halfway up the sides of the mold. Bake for 1 hour.

5. Remove the cake from the oven and let cool to room temperature in its mold on a wire rack. Chill in the refrigerator overnight until ready to serve.

6. To serve, unmold the cake and place on a chilled dessert plate. Garnish with whipped cream, fresh fruit, and a mint leaf.

# Dark Chocolate
# Pudding Soufflé

YIELD: 8 SERVINGS

4 ounces/120g bittersweet (not unsweetened)
  chocolate, chopped
4 tablespoons/60g unsalted butter
4 large eggs, separated

⅓ cup/90g sugar
2 teaspoons coffee extract
¼ cup/40g confectioners' sugar

1. Preheat the oven to 350°F/180°C. Lightly butter eight 4-ounce/120g soufflé dishes or ramekins. Dust the molds with sugar, tilting to coat and tapping out the excess.

2. Place the chocolate and butter in the top of a double boiler set over 1 inch/2.5cm of simmering (not boiling) water. Whisk until the chocolate is smooth and no small lumps remain. Turn off the heat and remove the chocolate from the hot water. Set aside.

3. In a large mixing bowl, combine the egg yolks, sugar, and coffee extract. With an electric mixer, beat on high speed until pale in color, about 4 minutes, stopping 2 or 3 times to scrape down the sides of the bowl. Set aside.

4. Place the egg whites in a clean, grease-free mixing bowl. With an electric mixer, beat on low speed until frothy. Increase the speed to medium-high and beat until the whites hold stiff but not dry peaks.

5. Slowly fold the chocolate mixture into the egg yolks with a spatula until well blended. Fold in the egg whites until well combined, taking care not to deflate them. Fill the soufflé molds three-quarters full with the mixture and bake for 20 minutes, or until risen. Place the confectioners' sugar in a sieve and sprinkle it over the tops of the soufflés. Serve immediately.

# Chocolate Cake with Chocolate Ganache Frosting

YIELD: 12 SERVINGS

1 pound plus 10 ounces/744g bittersweet
(not unsweetened) chocolate, chopped

2 cups/500ml heavy cream

1 stick/120g unsalted butter, at room temperature

½ cup/120g sugar

5 large eggs, separated

3 ounces/90g almonds, ground

2 tablespoons dark rum

2 ½ cups/290g cake flour
Sliced strawberries for garnish

1. To make the ganache, place 1 pound/454g chocolate in a medium bowl. In a medium saucepan, bring the cream to a boil. As soon as it boils, pour the cream over the chocolate all at once. Whisk the mixture until it is smooth and no small lumps of chocolate remain. Let cool at room temperature, cover with plastic wrap, and chill in the refrigerator until firm and ready to use.

2. Preheat the oven to 300°F/150°C. Butter an 8-inch/20cm springform pan and line the bottom with a round of parchment paper.

3. Place the chocolate in the top of a double boiler set over 1 inch/2.5cm of simmering (not boiling) water. Whisk until the chocolate is smooth and no small lumps remain. Turn off the heat and leave the chocolate over the hot water. Set aside.

4. In a large mixing bowl, combine the butter and ¼ cup/60g sugar. With an electric mixer, beat until light and fluffy. Add the egg yolks and beat for 1 minute. Add the almonds and rum and beat for 2 more minutes, stopping 2 or 3 times to scrape down the sides of the bowl. Sift the flour over the batter. With a rubber spatula, fold the flour in gently. Set aside.

5. Place the egg whites in a clean, grease-free mixing bowl. With an electric mixer, beat on low speed until frothy. Increase the speed to medium and gradually add the remaining ¼ cup/60g sugar. When the sugar is incorporated, increase the speed to medium-high and beat until the whites hold stiff but not dry peaks.

6. Add the melted chocolate to the butter-sugar mixture. With a rubber spatula, fold the chocolate in until well combined. Spoon one-fourth of the egg whites into the chocolate mixture and gently mix until the batter is lightened somewhat. Fold in the remaining egg whites, taking care not to deflate them, until well combined.

7. Pour the batter into the prepared pan and bake for 25 to 30 minutes, or until a skewer inserted in the center comes out with some crumbs clinging to it. Remove from the oven and let cool in the pan on a wire rack. Run a sharp knife around the edge of the pan and remove the ring. Transfer the cake to a plate.

8. With an electric mixer, beat the chilled ganache on medium speed until light and fluffy. Smooth the ganache over the top and sides of the cake. Garnish with strawberries and serve at room temperature.

# Flourless Chocolate Cake with Fresh Fruit

YIELD: 10 SERVINGS

1 pound/454g semisweet chocolate, broken into pieces
1 tablespoon pure vanilla extract
1 tablespoon dark rum
¾ cup/200ml strong brewed coffee
8 large eggs

½ cup/120g sugar
¾ cup/200ml heavy cream
    Whipped cream, assorted fresh fruit, and mint
    leaves for garnish

1. Preheat the oven to 300°F/150°C. Butter a 12-inch/30cm terrine mold and refrigerate it until ready to use. Chill a large mixing bowl.

2. Place the chocolate, vanilla, rum, and coffee in the top of a double boiler set over 1 inch/2.5cm of simmering (not boiling) water. Whisk until the chocolate is smooth and no small lumps remain. Turn off the heat and remove the chocolate from the hot water. Transfer the mixture to a large bowl.

3. In a medium mixing bowl, combine the eggs and sugar. With an electric mixer, beat until pale in color, stopping 2 or 3 times to scrape down the sides of the bowl. Add some of the chocolate mixture and beat until incorporated. Pour this mixture into the remaining chocolate mixture. Stir until combined.

4. Bring a large kettle of water to a boil. In the chilled mixing bowl, whip the cream until soft peaks form. With a rubber spatula, fold the whipped cream into the chocolate mixture until just combined. Pour the mixture into the prepared terrine mold and cover with aluminum foil. Place in a roasting pan and pour enough boiling water into the pan to come halfway up the sides of the mold. Bake for 1 hour.

5. Remove the cake from the oven and let cool to room temperature in its mold on a wire rack. Chill in the refrigerator overnight until ready to serve.

6. To serve, unmold the cake and place on a chilled dessert plate. Garnish with whipped cream, fresh fruit, and a mint leaf.

# Chocolate-Almond Pudding with Kahlúa Sabayon

YIELD: 4 SERVINGS

## Kahlúa Sabayon

4  *large egg yolks*
3  *tablespoons sugar*

½  *cup/125ml Kahlúa*

1. Prepare a large bowl of ice water; set aside. In a wide saucepan, bring about 1 inch/2.5cm of water to a simmer. Adjust the heat so that the water is at a bare simmer. In a large heatproof mixing bowl that can sit on the pan, combine the egg yolks and sugar. With an electric mixer, beat on high speed until pale in color, about 3 minutes, stopping 2 or 3 times to scrape down the sides of the bowl. Whisk in the Kahlúa.

2. Set the bowl over the pan and whisk constantly until the mixture thickens and is lemony looking, about 3 minutes.

3. Remove the bowl from the heat and place it in the larger bowl of ice water to chill the sabayon quickly. When cool, cover with plastic wrap and chill in the refrigerator.

## Pudding

1  *cup/115g blanched almonds*
5  *tablespoons confectioners' sugar*
2  *ounces/60g semisweet chocolate*
3  *tablespoons/45g unsalted butter*

3  *large eggs, separated*
2  *tablespoons sugar*
1  *cup/250ml heavy cream*
   *Fresh fruit for garnish (optional)*

1. Preheat the oven to 350°F/180°C. Thoroughly coat a 1 quart/1 liter pudding mold with butter. Dust the mold with 2 tablespoons confectioners' sugar; tilt to coat and tap out the excess. Chill a large mixing bowl.

2. Spread the almonds on a baking sheet and bake for 5 to 7 minutes, or until fragrant. Let cool. Grind in a food processor or coffee grinder until finely ground. Leave the oven on.

3. Place the chocolate in the top of a double boiler set over 1 inch of simmering (not boiling) water. Whisk until the chocolate is smooth and no small lumps remain. Turn off the heat and remove the chocolate from the hot water. Set aside.

4. In a large mixing bowl, combine the butter and remaining 3 tablespoons confectioners' sugar. With an electric mixer, beat until light and fluffy. Add the egg yolks, one at a time, beating well after each addition. Add the chocolate and ground almonds and beat until well blended. Set aside.

5. Place the egg whites in a clean, grease-free mixing bowl. With an electric mixer, beat on low speed until frothy. Increase the speed to medium and gradually add the sugar. When the sugar is incorporated, increase the speed to medium-high and beat until the whites hold stiff but not dry peaks.

6. Spoon one-fourth of the egg whites into the chocolate mixture and gently mix until the batter is lightened somewhat. With a rubber spatula, fold in the remaining egg whites until well combined, making sure not to deflate them.

7. Bring a large kettle of water to a boil. Pour the mixture into the prepared mold and place in a roasting pan. Pour enough boiling water into the roasting pan to come halfway up the sides of the mold. Bake for 30 to 40 minutes, or until set.

8. Remove the mold from the water bath and let cool for 5 minutes on a wire rack. Meanwhile, in the chilled mixing bowl, whip the cream until stiff but still glossy. With a rubber spatula, fold ½ cup/125ml whipped cream into the chilled Kahlúa sabayon.

9. To serve, invert the pudding onto a platter and unmold it. Top with the Kahlúa sabayon. Garnish with the remaining whipped cream and fresh fruit if desired.

# Carrot-Nut Torte

YIELD: 8 SERVINGS

5 large egg whites
1 cup/225g sugar
7 large egg yolks, lightly beaten
2 cups/160g grated carrots
2 cups/230g pecans, walnuts, or almonds, toasted and chopped

½ cup/70g cornstarch
2 tablespoons/30g unsalted butter, melted
2 tablespoons fresh lemon juice
¾ cup/100g confectioners' sugar

1. Preheat the oven to 350°F/180°C. Coat a 9-inch/23cm springform pan with butter. Dust the pan with a little flour; tilt to coat and tap out the excess.

2. Place the egg whites in a clean, grease-free mixing bowl. With an electric mixer, beat on low speed until frothy, 2 to 3 minutes. Increase the speed to medium and gradually add the sugar. When the sugar is incorporated, increase the speed to medium-high and beat until the whites hold stiff but not dry peaks, 2 to 3 minutes.

3. Place the egg yolks in the bowl of an electric mixer. Beat on high speed for 5 minutes, or until pale yellow in color. With a rubber spatula, fold the yolks into the egg whites until well combined, taking care not to deflate the whites.

4. In a medium bowl, combine the carrots, nuts, and cornstarch. Carefully fold the mixture into the eggs. Blend in the butter and lemon juice.

5. Pour the batter into the prepared pan and bake for 40 minutes, or until a skewer inserted in the center comes out clean. Transfer the pan to a wire rack and let cool completely before serving.

6. Run a sharp knife around the edge of the pan and remove the ring. Transfer the cake to a plate. Place the confectioners' sugar in a sieve and sprinkle it over the torte.

# Banana-Apple Bread Pudding with Banana-Rum Sauce

YIELD: 8 TO 10 SERVINGS

## Bread Pudding

6 cups/360g day-old French baguette, torn into bite-size pieces
½ cup/50g pecans
3 large eggs
3 cups/750ml whole milk
⅔ cup/160g sugar
2 large ripe bananas

3 apples, peeled, cored, and roughly chopped
1 ½ teaspoons ground cinnamon
⅛ teaspoon ground nutmeg
½ teaspoon pure vanilla extract
½ cup/60g raisins
3 tablespoons/45g unsalted butter, cut into small pieces

## nutmeg

A whiff of this spice brings many of us home for the holidays, back to eggnog and pumpkin pie, warm hugs, and jovial thumps on the back. Now that you are a grown-up, nutmeg may bring new pleasure to familiar comfort foods, for it is a powerful aphrodisiac. Nefzawí prescribed a mixture of nutmeg and honey (and "incense") to men who experienced their pleasure a few minutes too soon. Nutmeg also causes a delicious fervor in women. Like many spices, nutmeg in excessive amounts is toxic. But a sprinkle or two should take you both where you most want to go.

1. Preheat the oven to 300°F/150°C. Coat a 12-by-9-inch/30-by-23cm baking dish with butter. Place the bread pieces in the dish and set aside. Spread the pecans on a baking sheet and bake for 5 to 7 minutes, or until fragrant. Let cool, chop, and set aside.

2. In a food processor, combine the eggs, milk, sugar, bananas, apples, cinnamon, nutmeg, and vanilla. Process until thoroughly blended. Pour the mixture over the bread pieces and sprinkle with the raisins and pecans. With a rubber spatula, gently mix the raisins and nuts into the pudding. Let the pudding sit for 20 minutes.

3. Meanwhile, bring a large kettle of water to a boil. Dot the pudding with the butter and cover it with aluminum foil. Place the baking dish in a larger roasting pan and pour enough boiling water into the pan to come halfway up the sides of the baking dish. Bake for 1 hour and remove the foil. Bake for an additional 15 minutes and remove from the oven.

## Banana-Rum Sauce

⅔ cup/150g unsalted butter, softened
½ cup/100g packed light brown sugar
3 large ripe bananas, sliced lengthwise and crosswise to make 4 pieces each
¼ teaspoon ground cinnamon

⅛ teaspoon ground nutmeg
3 tablespoons dark rum
2 tablespoons banana liqueur
½ teaspoon pure vanilla extract

1. In a large skillet, melt the butter over low heat. Add the brown sugar, bananas, cinnamon, and nutmeg. Moving the skillet back and forth, cook until the butter and sugar become creamy and the bananas begin to soften, about 1 minute.

2. Remove the skillet from the stove and add the rum and the banana liqueur. While carefully standing back, return the skillet to the stove and tilt it slightly away from the body to ignite the alcohol. (If you do not have a gas stove, hold a match at the edge of the skillet and tilt it slightly away from the body.) Move the skillet back and forth constantly until the flames die out. Add the vanilla and remove from the heat.

**To Assemble**

¾ cup/200ml heavy cream

1 tablespoon sugar

¼ teaspoon pure vanilla extract

2 bananas, peeled and cut into at least 16 slices

1. In a chilled large mixing bowl, whip the cream until slightly thickened. While whipping, gradually add the sugar and vanilla. Continue whipping until the sugar is incorporated and soft peaks form.

2. To serve, place a piece of warm bread pudding on a plate. Top with 2 slices of banana and some of the banana-rum sauce. Garnish with a dollop of whipped cream and serve immediately.

---

# Baked Bananas en Papillote

YIELD: 2 SERVINGS

2 ripe bananas, peeled

1 vanilla bean, split

2 tablespoons dark rum

1. Preheat the oven to 425°F/220°C. Place each banana on a large square of aluminum foil. Scrape the blade of a blunt knife along the inside of the vanilla bean to remove the seeds. Place a vanilla bean half and its seeds next to each banana. Drizzle 1 tablespoon rum over each banana and roll up loosely in the foil, sealing the ends. Place the packages on a baking sheet and bake for 20 minutes.

2. To serve, open the edge and serve in the foil, as pictured opposite. Alternatively, remove the bananas from the foil and discard the vanilla beans. Divide the bananas between 2 glasses or plates. Place a scoop of vanilla ice cream alongside and top with chocolate sauce (page 154).

# bananas

This humble fruit—one of the first cultivated by man—combines tropical exoticism with the homeyness of comfort food. Arabs introduced this ancient Asian native to Egypt by the year 700; Europeans later brought it to the New World, where it proliferates today. Bananas have an unrivaled sunny disposition; they are easily digested, high in potassium and vitamin B6, inexpensive, and endlessly versatile. There are more than 400 distinct varieties, ranging from creamy yellow to burnished red, from petite to nine inches long. And whether it is their phallic shape or their air of lighthearted humor, many swear that bananas inspire them to monkey around. The kiddies may smear them with peanut butter, but you and your mate will enjoy pairing them with smoother pleasures like vanilla ice cream and chocolate sauce or with tangy fruits such as oranges, kumquats, and pineapple. And if dessert doesn't lead to outright Tarzan-and-Jane role playing, you can be certain it will lead to other satisfying games. No wonder consumption is a robust 25 pounds/11.4kg per person in the United States.

# Banana-Pistachio Strudel
# with Rum-Raisin Sauce

YIELD: 4 SERVINGS

¼ cup/60ml light rum
½ cup/60g golden raisins
2 cups/500ml half-and-half
1 vanilla bean, split
½ cup/120g sugar
4 large egg yolks

1 teaspoon ground cinnamon
1 teaspoon sugar
5 sheets phyllo dough (18 by 14 inches/46 by 35cm)
1 to 2 sticks/120 to 225g unsalted butter, melted
4 ripe bananas, peeled, split lengthwise, and sliced
½ cup/65g chopped pistachios

1. To make the rum-raisin sauce, gently warm the rum in a small saucepan over medium heat or in the microwave on medium power. In a small bowl, combine with the raisins. Marinate for at least 30 minutes.

2. In a medium saucepan, bring the half-and-half to a boil. Reduce the heat to low and use the tip of a blunt knife to scrape the vanilla bean seeds into the half-and-half. Gently simmer, stirring occasionally, until the vanilla has infused the half-and-half, about 15 minutes.

3. Meanwhile, in a mixing bowl, whisk the sugar and egg yolks until light colored. Slowly pour half of the half-and-half into the egg yolk mixture, gently whisking until well blended.

4. Prepare a large bowl of ice water. Return the egg yolk mixture to the saucepan and place over medium-low heat. Gently cook, stirring continually with a wooden spoon, until the mixture thickens and coats the back of the spoon and an instant-read thermometer registers 185°F/85°C. (The mixture should not be allowed to boil.) Immediately remove the mixture from the heat and strain through a fine sieve into a medium bowl. Place the bowl in the larger bowl of ice water to chill the mixture quickly and prevent curdling.

5. When the mixture is cool, stir in the rum-raisin marinade. Cover and chill until ready to use.

6. To make the strudel, preheat the oven to 350°F/180°C. Lightly coat a baking sheet with butter. In a small bowl, combine the cinnamon and sugar.

7. Lay 1 sheet of phyllo on a work surface. (Keep the remaining phyllo covered with plastic wrap and a damp kitchen towel.) With a pastry brush, brush the phyllo sheet lightly with some melted butter. Lay another sheet of phyllo on top. Lightly brush with more butter and sprinkle with 1 teaspoon cinnamon sugar. Lay a third sheet of phyllo on top. Lightly brush with more butter and the remaining cinnamon sugar. Repeat the phyllo and butter layers with the remaining 2 sheets of phyllo, ending with the top sheet buttered.

8. Spread the sliced bananas on the top phyllo sheet and sprinkle with the pistachios. Starting from a long edge, roll up the phyllo into a cylinder. Brush with melted butter. Place on the prepared baking sheet and bake for 15 to 20 minutes, or until golden. Remove from the oven and let cool for 10 minutes.

9. To serve, transfer the strudel to a cutting board and slice into 4 diagonal slices. Serve with the rum-raisin sauce on top.

# Baked Apples with Sabayon and Strawberry Sauce

Yield: 2 servings

### Strawberry Sauce

¼ pound/120g fresh strawberries, washed and hulled
½ cup/70g confectioners' sugar

2 tablespoons fresh orange juice
½ tablespoon fresh lemon juice

In a blender or food processor, puree the strawberries until smooth. Strain through a fine sieve into a bowl. Add the confectioners' sugar and stir until dissolved. Whisk in the orange juice and lemon juice. Cover and chill in the refrigerator until needed.

### Baked Apples

2 tablespoons chopped walnuts
2 tablespoons raisins
2 teaspoons brown sugar

2 Gala apples, cored
2 teaspoons unsalted butter, softened

Preheat the oven to 350°F/180°C. Prepare a mixture of walnuts, raisins, and brown sugar and fill in the cored hole of each apple. Place 1 teaspoon of butter in each apple on top of the mixture. Place the apples in a baking dish and bake until tender, 20 to 30 minutes.

### Sabayon

1 large egg
3 large egg yolks
2 tablespoons sugar
3 tablespoons dry white wine

2 tablespoons unsweetened apple juice
1 teaspoon cornstarch
2 teaspoons ground cinnamon
2 sprigs mint

1. In a wide saucepan, bring about 1 inch/2.5cm of water to a simmer. Adjust the heat so that the water is at a bare simmer. In a large heatproof mixing bowl that can sit on the saucepan, combine the egg, egg yolks, and sugar. With an electric mixer, beat on high speed until pale in color, about 3 minutes, stopping 2 or 3 times to scrape down the sides of the bowl. Whisk in the wine and apple juice.

2. Set the bowl over the pan and whisk constantly until the mixture thickens and is lemony looking, about 3 minutes.

3. Remove the bowl from the heat, sift the cornstarch over the mixture, and continue beating until just incorporated.

4. Swirl the strawberry sauce on each plate and top with a baked apple. Spoon the sabayon over the apples. Place the cinnamon in a fine sieve and sprinkle it over the sabayon. Garnish with a mint sprig and serve immediately.

## apples

Across Europe, the fruit's original home, apples are the stuff of romantic legend. Ancient Scandinavians believed apples to be the rejuvenating food of the gods, and ancient Greek lovers exchanged them as presents. In medieval Germany a woman who steeped an apple in her own perspiration and then fed it to her lover could expect to become irresistible. Scholars today debate the likelihood of Adam and Eve's apple transgression—not whether they ate the forbidden fruit but whether that fruit was actually an apple. Until the issue has been settled, there is no harm in sharing—unabashedly unclothed, of course—one of these ripe fruits in your own garden or bedroom.

# Baked Alaska

YIELD: 6 SERVINGS

### Chocolate Ice Cream

4  cups/1l whole milk
7  ounces/200g unsweetened chocolate, chopped

1 ½  cups/345g sugar
8  large egg yolks

1. In a medium heavy saucepan, bring the milk to a boil. Reduce the heat to low, add the chocolate, and simmer, stirring occasionally, until the chocolate is smooth and no small lumps remain. Keep warm.

2. Meanwhile, in a mixing bowl, whisk the sugar and egg yolks until lightly colored. Slowly pour half of the warm chocolate milk into the egg yolk mixture, gently whisking until well blended.

3. Prepare a large bowl of ice water. Return the egg yolk mixture to the saucepan and place over medium-low heat. Gently cook, stirring continually with a wooden spoon, until the mixture thickens and coats the back of the spoon and an instant-read thermometer registers 185°F/85°C. (The mixture should not be allowed to boil.) Immediately remove the mixture from the heat and strain through a fine sieve into a medium bowl. Place the bowl in the larger bowl of ice water to chill the mixture quickly and prevent curdling.

4. When the mixture is cool, cover and chill in the refrigerator until cold. Spoon the mixture into an ice cream maker and freeze according to the manufacturer's instructions. Transfer to a container; cover and freeze until ready to use.

### Ginger Ice Cream

2  cups/500ml whole milk
One 2-inch/5cm piece fresh ginger, peeled and sliced

½  cup/120g sugar
6  large egg yolks

1. In a medium nonreactive saucepan, bring the milk to a boil. Reduce the heat to low and add the ginger slices. Gently simmer, stirring occasionally, until the ginger has infused the milk, about 15 minutes.

2. Meanwhile, in a mixing bowl, whisk the sugar and egg yolks until lightly colored. Slowly pour half of the ginger-infused milk into the egg yolk mixture, gently whisking until well blended.

3. Prepare a large bowl of ice water. Return the egg yolk mixture to the saucepan and place over medium-low heat. Gently cook, stirring continually with a wooden spoon, until the mixture thickens and coats the back of the spoon and an instant-read thermometer registers 185°F/85°C. (The mixture should not be allowed to boil.) Immediately remove the mixture from the heat and strain through a fine sieve into a medium bowl. Place the bowl in the larger bowl of ice water to chill the mixture quickly and prevent curdling.

4. When the mixture is cool, cover and chill in the refrigerator until cold. Spoon the mixture into an ice cream maker and freeze according to the manufacturer's instructions. Transfer to a container; cover and freeze until ready to use.

## Cake

¾ cup/150g firmly packed sweetened almond paste
¼ cup/60g sugar
9 tablespoons/135g unsalted butter
3 large eggs

1 tablespoon Grand Marnier (optional)
⅓ cup/40g cake flour
Pinch salt

1. Preheat the oven to 350°F/180°C. Butter a 10-inch/25cm springform pan and line the bottom with a round of parchment paper.

2. In a medium mixing bowl, combine the almond paste, sugar, and butter. With an electric mixer, beat until light and fluffy and until most of the sugar has been incorporated, about 2 minutes. Add the eggs, one at a time, beating well after each addition. With a wooden spoon, stir in the remaining ingredients and mix until just combined. (Do not overmix.)

3. Pour the batter into the prepared pan and bake for 15 to 20 minutes, or until the top is light golden and springs back when pressed lightly. Remove from the oven and let cool in the pan on a wire rack. When completely cool, unmold and remove the parchment paper. With a 3-inch/7.5cm cookie cutter, cut 6 rounds from the cake layer and place them on a parchment-lined baking sheet.

4. With an ice cream scoop, place 1 or 2 balls of ice cream in any flavor combination on each cake round. Cover and freeze until very hard, about 45 minutes.

## Italian Meringue

3 large egg whites
¾ cup/170g sugar

¼ cup/60ml water

1. Place the egg whites in a clean, grease-free mixing bowl. With an electric mixer, beat on low speed until frothy. Increase the speed to medium-high and beat until the whites hold stiff but not dry peaks.

2. In a small heavy saucepan, combine the sugar and water over medium heat. Bring to a boil and cook

without stirring until a candy thermometer registers 250°F/120°C (soft-ball stage). Immediately remove from the heat and very slowly pour into the egg whites, beating continuously, making sure to avoid pouring the syrup on the beaters. Continue beating until the bottom of the mixing bowl is warm but not hot to the touch, about 5 minutes.

## To Assemble

1. Preheat the oven to 450°F/230°C. Using a pastry bag fitted with a ¾-inch/1.9cm plain tip, decorate the reserved ice cream–topped cake rounds with the meringue. Return the decorated slices to the freezer for 15 minutes.

2. To serve, bake the desserts in the oven for 2 to 3 minutes, until the meringue begins to turn golden. Remove from the oven and serve immediately.

# cakes

Medieval maidens of northern Europe lured their beaux with spice cakes baked in small ovens over their own naked bodies. Sometimes an older woman would balance the small oven on a wooden plank atop the love-hungry lady's midsection so her own passionate heat would ignite a flame in him who ate the sweet. Even more to the point, others imprinted their intentions onto bread dough by pressing it against their vulva before baking. Cockle bread no doubt earned its name from its bold imprinted seashell pattern. Today's woman might allude to her own sexy shape by making baked Alaska, each one an elegant breast.

# Apple Pie

YIELD: ONE 9-INCH/23CM DEEP-DISH PIE

2 cups/240g all-purpose flour

½ cup/65g ground almonds

1 teaspoon sugar

¾ teaspoon salt

½ teaspoon ground cinnamon

1 stick/120g cold unsalted butter, cut into pieces

⅓ cup/75g cold vegetable shortening, cut into pieces

4 to 5 tablespoons whole milk

3 pounds/1.4kg local pie apples, peeled, cored, and sliced (about 9 apples)

½ cup/120g sugar

2 tablespoons fresh lemon juice

¾ teaspoon ground cinnamon

2 tablespoons all-purpose flour

1 tablespoon/15g unsalted butter, cut into small pieces

1. Combine the flour, almonds, sugar, salt, and cinnamon in a large bowl. Add the butter and shortening to the flour mixture and work them in with your fingers until the mixture resembles coarse crumbs.

2. Add the milk, using only as much as needed to gather the mixture into a soft ball of dough. Cut the dough in half and flatten each half into a disk. Cover the dough with plastic wrap and let it rest at least 30 minutes.

3. Preheat the oven to 375°F/190°C. Combine the apples, sugar, lemon juice, cinnamon, and flour in a large bowl. Toss the ingredients to coat all the apple slices.

4. Lightly flour a pastry board or clean work surface. Roll one disk of dough on the floured surface into a round ⅛ inch/3mm thick, making sure the round is larger than the pie pan by about an inch.

5. Place the dough in a 9-inch/23cm deep-dish pie pan. Pour the apple filling into the dough-lined pan. Dot the top of the filling with the butter. Roll out the remaining dough and place it over the filling. Gather the edges of the bottom and top crusts together, roll them gently, then press the dough onto the rim of the pie pan. Crimp the edge with your fingers or press it with the tines of a fork.

6. Bake the pie for 50 to 60 minutes, or until the pastry is golden brown. Serve with vanilla ice cream if desired.

# Fudge-Walnut Brownies

YIELD: 12 SERVINGS

6   ounces/180g bittersweet (not unsweetened)
    chocolate, chopped
1   cup/225g unsalted butter
2   cups/454g sugar
5   large eggs

¾   cup/100g all-purpose flour
¼   cup/20g unsweetened cocoa powder
2   tablespoons pure vanilla extract
½   teaspoon salt
1   cup/115g coarsely chopped walnuts

1. Preheat the oven to 375°F/190°C. Coat a 13-by-9-inch/33-by-23cm baking dish with butter. Dust the dish with a little flour; tilt to coat and tap out the excess.

2. Place the chocolate in the top of a double boiler set over 1 inch of simmering (not boiling) water. Whisk until the chocolate is smooth and no small lumps remain. Turn off the heat and remove the chocolate from the hot water. Set aside.

3. In a large mixing bowl, combine the butter and sugar. With an electric mixer, beat at medium speed until light and fluffy, 6 to 8 minutes. Add the eggs, one at a time, beating well after each addition. With a wooden spoon, stir in the remaining ingredients.

4. Pour the batter into the prepared pan and bake for 25 minutes, or until a skewer inserted in the center comes out clean. Let cool for about an hour before cutting into squares and serving.

# Coffee-Rum Cookies
# with Almonds

YIELD: 1 DOZEN COOKIES

1    stick/120g cold unsalted butter
1    cup/225g sugar
1    large egg
2 ¼  cups/270g all-purpose flour
2    tablespoons strong brewed coffee

¼    cup/60ml dark rum
1    tablespoon baking powder
     Pinch salt
½    cup/58g finely chopped almonds

1. In a large mixing bowl, combine the butter and sugar. With an electric mixer, beat until fluffy. In another bowl, whisk the egg, ¼ cup/30g flour, coffee, and rum. Add the egg mixture to the butter mixture and beat until fully incorporated, stopping 2 or 3 times to scrape down the sides of the bowl.

2. In a medium bowl, whisk the remaining 2 cups/240g flour, baking powder, salt, and almonds. Slowly add to the wet ingredients, beating on low speed until just combined, 3 to 4 minutes. Cover with plastic wrap and chill in the refrigerator until firm, about 1 hour.

3. Preheat the oven to 350°F/180°C. On a lightly floured surface, roll out the dough ⅛ inch/3mm thick. Cut out shapes with a cookie cutter and place on ungreased baking sheets. Bake in batches for 8 to 10 minutes, or until light golden brown on the bottom. Transfer to a wire rack and let cool for 20 to 30 minutes.

## coffee

When the Inkspots recorded their R&B hit "The Java Jive" back in 1956, could they have foreseen the love affair Americans would have with "joe" at the turn of the century? By now you know that coffee's jolt comes from caffeine, an alkaloid also found in tea, kola nuts, and chocolate (in a relatively small amount). Coffee perks you up, sparks stimulating conversation—an overlooked aphrodisiac—and fills the room with its mellow, bitter bouquet. Adding a bit of cream creates a sudden swirl of rich browns. One sip warms the lips, mouth, and throat. If coffee were not so widely loved, it would not be the object of so much scientific study: Linked to cancer or longevity? Chemical- or water-based decaffeination? Aphrodisiac or inhibitor? Above all, moderation is the key. You want to be awake and aroused to enjoy each other's company, but not so nervous that your pulse is racing. If you want to raise your pulse, I think you can find another way.

# Pecan Chocolate Chip Cookies

2 sticks/454g unsalted butter, at room temperature
¼ cup/60g sugar
⅓ cup/75g packed light brown sugar
2 large eggs
1 teaspoon pure vanilla extract

1 ¾ cups/320g all-purpose flour
Pinch salt
1 teaspoon baking soda
1 cup/100g pecans, chopped
8 ounces/225g chocolate chips

1. In a large mixing bowl, combine the butter, sugar, and brown sugar. With an electric mixer, beat on low-medium speed until well blended, 3 to 4 minutes. Add the eggs and vanilla and beat until fully incorporated, stopping 2 or 3 times to scrape down the sides of the bowl.

2. In a medium bowl, whisk the flour, salt, and baking soda. Slowly add to the wet ingredients, beating until just combined. Add the pecans and chocolate chips and beat until just mixed. Cover with plastic wrap and chill in the refrigerator until firm, about 1 hour.

3. Preheat the oven to 325°F/160°C. Drop tablespoons of the dough 2 inches apart onto 2 baking sheets. Bake in batches for 8 to 10 minutes, or until light brown on the bottom. Transfer the cookies to a wire rack to cool for 20 to 30 minutes. Serve warm.

# Figs in Red Wine with Mint Sabayon

YIELD: 4 SERVINGS

### Marinated Figs

10 fresh figs, washed, stemmed, and halved lengthwise
½ cup/125ml water
1 ½ cups/375ml red Burgundy wine
1 tablespoon red wine vinegar
⅞ cup/200g sugar
1 teaspoon grated fresh ginger

Zest of ¼ lemon
Zest of ½ orange
1 cinnamon stick
¼ vanilla bean, split
5 cloves

1. Arrange the figs, cut side up, in a 13-by-9-inch/ 33-by-23cm baking dish. Set aside.

2. In a large saucepan over medium heat, combine the remaining ingredients and bring to a boil. Reduce the heat to low and simmer gently, stirring occasionally, until the citrus peel is tender, about 10 minutes. Remove from the heat.

3. Pour the liquid over the figs and cover. Let stand at room temperature for 3 hours or chill in the refrigerator overnight.

### Mint Sabayon

3 large egg yolks, at room temperature
3 tablespoons Riesling wine

2 tablespoons sugar
2 tablespoons chopped fresh mint

1. In a wide saucepan, bring about 1 inch of water to a simmer. Adjust the heat so that the water is at a bare simmer. In a large heatproof mixing bowl that can sit on the saucepan, combine the egg yolks, wine, and sugar. With an electric mixer, beat until pale in color, stopping 2 or 3 times to scrape down the sides of the bowl.

2. Set the bowl over the pan and whisk constantly until the mixture thickens and is lemony looking. Stir in the mint. Remove the bowl from the heat.

3. To serve, arrange 5 marinated fig halves, cut side up, in each of 4 soup plates. Spoon some of the marinade around the figs. Spoon some sabayon over the figs and serve immediately.

## wine

The naturally fermented juice of grapes has sustained and gladdened the human race since the first hunters and gatherers discovered it—probably by accident. Phoenician traders brought wine to Europe via Mediterranean trade routes. By the time the ancient Greek and Roman civilizations were established, wine had influenced practically every aspect of Western culture, including government, religion, medicine, and agriculture. The pleasures of wine—color, aroma, and taste—are endlessly fascinating, and its study includes geography, botany, and chemistry. In other words, wine is as complicated and engaging as love itself, and the two are best experienced together. Both are subjective. As a splendid wine triggers a glow in the mouth, the throat, and beyond, true love resonates throughout your whole being. Neither one is explainable. The final word in choosing wine is always to let instinct guide you; make sure to find a wine you love. Swirl, sniff, savor, and swallow it. And *share* it. With the one you love.

# Floating Islands on Crème Anglaise

YIELD: 4 SERVINGS

3  large egg whites
   Pinch cream of tartar
1  tablespoon sugar plus 1 ½ cups/345g
3  cups/750ml whole milk

½  vanilla bean, split
4  large egg yolks
8  tablespoons water

1. Place the egg whites and cream of tartar in a clean, grease-free mixing bowl. With an electric mixer, beat on low speed until frothy. Increase the speed to medium and gradually add 1 tablespoon sugar. When the sugar is incorporated, increase the speed to medium-high and beat until the whites hold stiff, glossy peaks.

2. In a medium saucepan, combine the milk and vanilla bean over medium-low heat. Bring to a gentle simmer.

3. Spoon or pipe with a pastry bag some of the beaten egg whites into egg shapes onto the surface of the milk, being careful that they don't touch one another. Allow the islands to steam on the simmering milk until set, about 4 minutes. Using a slotted spoon, remove the islands and place on a clean kitchen towel. Repeat with the remaining egg whites. Reserve the vanilla-infused milk for the crème anglaise.

4. To make the crème anglaise, whisk ½ cup/120g sugar and egg yolks until lightly colored in a mixing bowl. Slowly pour 2 cups of the reserved vanilla-infused milk into the egg yolk mixture, gently whisking until well blended.

5. Prepare a large bowl of ice water. Return the milk mixture to the saucepan and place over medium-low heat. Gently cook, stirring continually with a wooden spoon, until the mixture thickens and coats the back of the spoon and an instant-read thermometer registers 185°F/85°C. Immediately remove the sauce from the heat and strain through a fine sieve into a medium bowl. Place the bowl in the larger bowl of ice water to chill the sauce quickly and prevent curdling. When cool, cover with plastic wrap and chill in the refrigerator.

6. Lightly coat a baking sheet with butter. In a small saucepan, combine the remaining sugar and water over medium heat. Bring to a boil and cook without stirring until the syrup turns golden. Immediately drizzle the syrup decoratively onto the prepared baking sheet to make 4 caramel garnishes. Let cool completely.

7. To serve, ladle some crème anglaise into each of 4 soup plates. Float 2 or 3 islands in each plate. Garnish with caramel and serve.

# Assorted Sorbets

YIELD: 4 SERVINGS

### Mango Sorbet

*2 large mangoes, peeled and pitted, the pits reserved*
*1 ½ cups/375ml water*

*¾ cup/170g sugar*
*3 tablespoons fresh lime juice*

1. In a food processor, puree the mangoes until smooth.

2. In a medium nonreactive saucepan, combine the mango pits, water, and sugar over medium heat. Bring to a boil and then strain into a bowl. Let cool to room temperature. Add the lime juice and mango puree and stir until incorporated. Cover and chill in the refrigerator until cold.

3. Transfer the mixture to an ice cream maker and freeze according to the manufacturer's instructions. Transfer to a bowl; cover and freeze until ready to use.

### Chocolate Sorbet

*1 ½ cups/345g sugar*
*4 cups/1l water*

*4 ounces/120g unsweetened chocolate, finely chopped*

1. In a medium saucepan over low heat, dissolve the sugar in the water. Add the chocolate and stir until thoroughly blended. Transfer to a bowl, cover, and chill in the refrigerator until cold.

2. Transfer the mixture to an ice cream maker and freeze according to the manufacturer's instructions. Transfer to a bowl; cover and freeze until ready to use.

### To Assemble

*4 ounces/120g semisweet chocolate, finely chopped*

1. Place the chocolate in the top of a double boiler set over 1 inch/2.5cm of simmering (not boiling) water. Whisk until the chocolate is smooth (do not boil the chocolate). Turn off the heat and remove the chocolate from the hot water.

2. When the chocolate has cooled, place it back over the warm (not simmering) water. Spoon the sorbets onto chilled dessert plates or in bowls. Dip a dessert spoon into the chocolate sauce and allow it to drizzle on the sorbets.

# Mascarpone-Mint Ice Cream with Vanilla-Lemon Syrup

YIELD: 2 SERVINGS

### Mascarpone-Mint Ice Cream

1 ¾ cups/395g sugar
3 cups/750g water
1 pound mascarpone cheese

3 tablespoons fresh lemon juice
15 fresh mint leaves, chopped

1. In a medium saucepan over medium heat, dissolve the sugar in the water. Bring to a boil and immediately remove from the heat. Add the mascarpone, lemon juice, and mint. Stir until thoroughly blended. Cover and chill in the refrigerator overnight.

2. The next day, strain the mixture through a fine sieve and spoon it into an ice cream maker. Freeze according to the manufacturer's instructions. You will have leftover ice cream.

### Vanilla-Lemon Syrup

½ cup/120g sugar
¼ cup/60ml water

2 vanilla beans, split
Fresh lemon juice to taste

1. In a medium saucepan over medium heat, combine the sugar, water, and vanilla beans. Bring to a boil and immediately remove from the heat. Allow to cool to room temperature.

2. Remove the vanilla beans from the syrup. Using the tip of a blunt knife, scrape the vanilla bean seeds into the syrup.

### To Assemble

1 grapefruit, peeled, sectioned, and membranes removed
2 fresh figs, quartered

To serve, spoon some vanilla-lemon syrup on each plate and top with a scoop of ice cream. Garnish with the grapefruit sections and fig quarters and serve immediately.

## vanilla

Not so long ago, every woman's magazine in the United States announced that the scents to which the male libido reacts most favorably are the homey fragrances that waft from the kitchen—with vanilla at the top of the list. This prompted a plethora of new vanilla products from the cosmetics industry: perfumes, soaps, bubble baths, and lotions. Interestingly, however, the discovery did *not* lead to a heightened interest in vanilla as a culinary ingredient.

Vanilla beans are the pods of a climbing orchid grown in such places as Mexico, Madagascar, and Polynesia. The ripe beans are macerated, fermented, and cured for a full six months to make vanilla extract. To show your lover your true feelings, scoop out some of the actual beans and gently scrape them into desserts to create the kind of flecks found in sensually authentic vanilla ice cream. You can steep the beans in brandy to create your own after-dinner cordial, or store them in sugar to impart their exotic perfume to all your love treats.

# Cardamom Tea Sorbet

⅔ cup/160g sugar
4 cups/1l water
1 cup/250ml freshly brewed black tea

1 tablespoon cardamom seeds
2 teaspoons fresh lime juice
1 large egg white, beaten

1. In a medium saucepan, combine the sugar and water over medium heat. Bring to a boil; add the tea and cardamom seeds. Remove from the heat and let stand for 30 minutes.

2. Strain the mixture into a bowl and add the lime juice. Cover and chill in the refrigerator until cold.

3. Transfer the mixture to an ice cream maker and freeze according to the manufacturer's instructions, stopping halfway through to add the egg white. Transfer to a bowl, cover, and freeze until ready to use.

## cardamom

The Tunisian Sheik Umar ibn Muhammad al-Nefzawí prescribed cardamom in his Arabic love manual, *The Perfumed Garden*, written in the late fourteenth or early fifteenth century. He believed the spice could stir passion in healthy men and restore vigor to those who found themselves impotent as a result of either inertia or illness. The good sheik included cardamom in both savory and sweet recipes, as you may in your own love kitchen, adding cardamom to everything from barbecue sauce and pickles to coffee and pastries.

# Peach Compote with Lavender

½ cup/120g sugar
1¼ cups/310ml cold water
1 sprig lemon verbena plus extra for garnish
3 spikes lavender flowers plus extra for garnish

8 firm peaches, peeled, pitted, and sliced
1 teaspoon arrowroot dissolved in 1 tablespoon cold water

1. In a medium saucepan, combine the sugar and water over medium heat. Bring to a boil; reduce the heat and simmer for 5 minutes. Remove from the heat and add the lemon verbena sprig and the lavender spikes. Let stand for 30 minutes.

2. Remove the herbs from the syrup. Add the peaches and return to the heat. Simmer the peaches until the fruit is just tender, 3 to 4 minutes. With a slotted spoon, transfer the peaches to a glass bowl. Reserve the syrup.

3. Add the arrowroot mixture to the hot syrup and whisk until the syrup becomes clear. Remove from the heat and pour the syrup over the peaches. Let cool to room temperature, cover, and chill in the refrigerator until cold.

4. To serve, divide the compote among 6 chilled bowls and garnish with lemon verbena and lavender flowers.

## rosemary

Snippets of this aromatic herb have garnished far too many plates of late. Overzealous cooks, at home and in restaurants, have been hypnotized by rosemary's brash charm. This sturdy shrub from southern Europe has been used for centuries as a pharmaceutical and love token. Tradition once dictated that a groom be presented with a bouquet of rosemary the morning of his wedding. This explains the nurse's comment in *Romeo and Juliet*, "Doth not rosemary and Romeo begin both with a letter?" Indeed, Shakespeare knew his aphrodisiacs. But rosemary's bold pine-tree scent can come on too strong. Just as you would not wear head-to-toe hunting regalia at the beach or a full-length evening gown to a croquet match, you mustn't overpower, say, a delicate fish with rosemary. When you are feeling bold—and bold is good—add rosemary to foods that can stand up to its personality: pork, roasted potatoes, and pizza.

# Rosemary Ice Cream with Raspberries

YIELD: 4 SERVINGS

¼ cup/60ml white dessert wine, such as Sauternes
2 cups/454g sugar
7 sprigs rosemary, each about 4 inches long
½ vanilla bean, split

1 ½ cups/375ml heavy cream, chilled
3 large egg whites, at room temperature
½ cup/85g fresh raspberries

1. Place the wine, sugar, and rosemary in a small saucepan over medium heat. Use the tip of a blunt knife to scrape the vanilla bean seeds into the mixture and bring to a boil. Remove from the heat. Let the wine infuse for about 30 minutes—you should be able to smell the aroma.

2. Strain the wine through a fine sieve into a container. Cover and chill in the refrigerator for 1 hour.

3. In a chilled large mixing bowl, whip the cream until stiff but still glossy. Gradually whip in the cold flavored wine. Set aside.

4. Place the egg whites in a clean, grease-free mixing bowl. With an electric mixer, beat on low speed until frothy. Increase the speed to medium-high and beat until the whites hold stiff but not dry peaks.

5. With a rubber spatula, fold the egg whites into the cream until well combined. Spoon the mixture into an ice cream maker and freeze according to the manufacturer's instructions.

6. To serve, place a scoop of rosemary ice cream in the center of 4 chilled dessert bowls. Surround with the raspberries and serve immediately.

# Peach Crepes with Honey Sauce

YIELD: 2 SERVINGS

### Crepes

1 ½ cups/180g all-purpose flour
¾ cup/170g sugar
Pinch salt

3 large eggs
2 ¾ cups/700ml whole milk
6 tablespoons/90g unsalted butter

1. In a medium mixing bowl, combine the flour, sugar, and salt. Make a well in the center. Place the eggs in the well and stir from the center outward with a fork, as you would for fresh pasta. Add the milk and stir until smooth and well blended. Cover and chill in the refrigerator for at least 30 minutes.

2. In a small saucepan, heat 4 tablespoons/60g butter over medium-high heat. When the butter turns nut brown, immediately pour it into a small bowl.

3. Remove the crepe batter from the refrigerator and let it come to room temperature. Stir in the browned butter. In a small saucepan, melt the remaining 2 tablespoons/90g butter over medium heat. Immediately remove from the heat.

4. Preheat the oven to 200°F/95°C. Place a crepe pan or any light nonstick skillet over medium-high heat. With a pastry brush, coat the pan with some of the melted butter. With a small ladle, add a small amount of batter to the pan and swirl to coat the entire surface with a thin layer. When golden on the bottom, flip the crepe and cook for just a few seconds more. Transfer the crepe to a plate and repeat with the remaining batter, stacking the crepes as you go. Keep warm in the oven while making the sauce. You will have extra crepes.

### Honey Sauce and Filling

1 cup/250ml fresh grapefruit juice
3 tablespoons honey
¼ cup/60g sugar
½ cup/60ml water
Zest of 1 orange, cut into long julienne strips
2 tablespoons/30g unsalted butter

3 ripe yellow peaches, peeled and pitted, 2 cubed and 1 thinly sliced
1 tablespoon packed light brown sugar
8 spikes lavender flowers
2 sprigs mint
2 strawberries, washed, hulled, and halved

1. In a small nonreactive saucepan, combine the grapefruit juice and honey over medium heat. Bring to a simmer and reduce by one-fourth. Remove from the heat and let the sauce come to room temperature.

2. To make the filling, dissolve the sugar in the water in a small saucepan over medium heat. Bring to a boil; reduce the heat to low, add the orange zest and poach the zest gently for 5 minutes. Remove from the heat and let the zest cool in its poaching liquid.

3. In a large skillet, melt the butter over medium heat. Add the cubed peaches and cook, gently stirring, until heated through. Add the brown sugar and stir until dissolved. Stir in half the lavender and remove from the heat.

4. To serve, spoon some peach filling into the center of a crepe and roll into a cylinder. Repeat with the remaining filling. Spoon some honey sauce on each plate and top two lavender flowers. Garnish with the peach slices, mint, and strawberries and serve immediately.

## honey

For most adults this sacred, golden goo brings one thing to mind—and it's not Winnie the Pooh. Where there are flowers, there are bees to pollinate them; thus, to humankind's great delight, honey is found all over the world. The Egyptians, Greeks, and Romans all kept bees and knew the sensual pleasures of honey. Both Nefzawí, author of *The Perfumed Garden*, and Vatsayana, author of the *Kama Sutra*, based many aphrodisiac recipes on honey and often recommended drinking cupfuls at a time. Jews and Christians have long rhapsodized about a fertile land that floweth with milk and honey, and the Old and New Testaments refer to honey as a sweet sustainer of life. Modern nutritionists call it a physical and mental tonic, and some even assert that it may increase the production of sex hormones. You and your lover can experiment with distinctive types of honey from various plants such as clover (mild and nostalgic of childhood), wildflower (bold), acacia (delicate), and pine (pungent). Honey imparts lovely color and bouquet, making it a favorite sweetener. And I needn't remind you that massaging a drop of it onto the skin invites exploration with the lips.

# Linzer Torte

### Tart Dough

3 sticks/680g unsalted butter, chilled and cubed

1 cup/225g plus 2 tablespoons sugar

2 large eggs

6 ounces/180g hazelnuts, toasted and finely ground

3 ½ cups/400g all-purpose flour

1 teaspoon baking powder

¼ teaspoon pure vanilla extract

Cream the butter and sugar until light, about 10 minutes. Add the eggs, one at a time, beating until fully incorporated. Add the remaining ingredients and mix until combined. Pat into a 2-inch/5cm thick disk, wrap in plastic wrap, and refrigerate overnight.

### To Assemble

1 cup/250ml raspberry jam

Strawberries for garnish

1. Preheat the oven to 350°F/180°C. Remove the dough from the refrigerator and cut it into 2 pieces, one two-thirds the size of the other. Return the smaller piece to the refrigerator.

2. Use a rolling pin to roll the larger piece into a 12-inch/30cm round. Transfer the dough to a 10-inch/25cm nonstick tart pan (heart shaped if available) with a removable bottom. Press the dough into the tart pan and up the sides. Remove any excess dough by rolling the rolling pin over the top of the pan to make a nice clean cut.

3. Fill the tart with the raspberry jam. Remove the smaller piece of dough from the refrigerator and, using a rolling pin, roll it into a rectangle about 10 by 6 inches/25 by 15cm. Cut into 12 equal-size strips; lay 6 evenly spaced strips diagonally across the tart and another 6 strips in the opposite direction in a lattice pattern. Use the rolling pin to remove any excess dough by rolling it over the top of the pan.

4. Bake the tart until evenly golden brown, about 40 minutes. Let cool on a wire rack and unmold before serving. Garnish with strawberries.

# Peach Melba

YIELD: 2 SERVINGS

1 cup/170g raspberries
2 tablespoons sugar
2 large ripe peaches (any kind)
1 teaspoon chopped pecans
1 egg white

6 tablespoons crème fraîche (page 16)
2 tablespoons confectioners' sugar
1 teaspoon pure vanilla extract
4 scoops vanilla ice cream
2 sprigs mint

1. In a blender or food processor, puree the raspberries until smooth. Strain the puree through a fine sieve into a bowl. Add the sugar and stir until dissolved. Cover and chill in the refrigerator until needed.

2. In a medium saucepan, bring 1 quart/1l water to a boil. Meanwhile, prepare a large bowl of ice water. Plunge the peaches in the boiling water and leave them in just until the skin is loosened, about 30 seconds. With a slotted spoon, remove the peaches and place them in the ice water for 4 minutes. Slip off the skins and cut the peaches in half. Remove the pits and set aside.

3. Preheat the oven to 350°F/180°C. Spread the chopped pecans on a baking sheet and bake for 3 minutes, or until fragrant. Let cool and set aside.

4. Place the egg white in a clean, grease-free mixing bowl. With an electric mixer, whip on low speed until frothy. Increase the speed to medium-high and whip until stiff peaks form.

5. In a large bowl, whisk the crème fraîche, confectioners' sugar, and vanilla. With a rubber spatula, fold in the egg white until well combined, taking care not to deflate it.

6. To serve, place 2 scoops of vanilla ice cream in the bottom of a chilled soup plate or glass. Surround the ice cream with 2 peach halves. Drizzle the peaches with the raspberry sauce. Spoon a dollop of the crème fraîche mixture on top and sprinkle with the toasted pecans and a mint sprig. Serve immediately.

## peaches

Caress this downy member of the rose family and notice its sensual shape, reminiscent of the creviced curves of a woman. Note, too, its feminine blush—either demure or vampy—and most important, its alluring perfume. At the market, nose out the peaches that send you on an olfactory trip right to Georgia; it is those gloriously scented specimens that will ignite your lover's passion. Whether you feed them to each other plain or combined with cream, chocolate, or other fruits, you'll understand why the Chinese revere them as a symbol of long life and immortality.

# Poached Pears with Chocolate Sauce

YIELD: 2 SERVINGS

2 ripe pears, peeled and cored
1 tablespoon fresh lemon juice
½ cup/125ml water
2 tablespoons honey

1 vanilla bean, split
2 scoops vanilla ice cream
½ cup/125ml chocolate sauce (recipe below)

1. Preheat the oven to 350°F/180°C. Place the pears in a large baking dish.

2. In a medium saucepan, combine the lemon juice, water, and honey over low heat. Use the tip of a blunt knife to scrape the vanilla bean seeds into the liquid. Bring the mixture to a slow boil, stirring occasionally.

3. After the mixture has boiled, pour it over the pears. Place the pears in the oven and bake until tender, basting 2 or 3 times with the cooking liquid.

4. Remove the pears from the oven and let cool to room temperature in their liquid. Cover and chill in the refrigerator until cold.

5. To serve, place a scoop of vanilla ice cream in the center of a dessert plate. Place a pear on the middle of the plate. Drizzle with the chocolate sauce. Alternatively, sprinkle with some pistachios or freshly chopped mint. Serve immediately.

## Chocolate Sauce

YIELD: 1 ½ CUPS/375ML

10 ounces/290g bittersweet (not unsweetened) chocolate, chopped

½ cup/125ml whole milk, plus extra if needed
½ teaspoon pure vanilla extract

Place the chocolate and milk in the top of a double boiler set over 1 inch/2.5cm of simmering (not boiling) water. Whisk until the mixture is smooth and no small lumps of chocolate remain. Remove the pan from the heat and stir in the vanilla. If the sauce looks too thick or curdled, add a little more milk. Serve warm or at room temperature. The sauce will keep, covered, in the refrigerator for up to 1 week.

# Raspberry Gratin

YIELD: 2 SERVINGS

4  large egg yolks
¼  cup/60ml champagne (any kind)
¼  cup/60g superfine sugar

2  cups/340g raspberries
   Chopped fresh mint for garnish

1. Place the egg yolks, champagne, and sugar in a large heatproof mixing bowl set over simmering water. Use a whisk or a hand-held electric beater to whip the mixture until very light in color, tripled in volume, and very thick. Keep the mixture over the simmering water as you whisk.

2. To serve, preheat the broiler. Place the raspberries on a flameproof dessert plate. Spoon the sauce over the raspberries. Place the plate under the broiler and heat until the sauce turns golden brown. (Alternatively, use a kitchen blowtorch to glaze the sauce.) Remove from the broiler and top with chopped mint. Feed this dessert to your partner with a spoon—or with a kiss.

---

# Seared Figs with Brandy

YIELD: 4 SERVINGS

1  tablespoon/15g unsalted butter
8  ripe black figs, stemmed and halved
1  tablespoon sugar
⅓  cup/75ml fresh orange juice

¼  teaspoon grated orange zest
1 ½  tablespoons brandy
4  scoops vanilla ice cream

1. In a large skillet, melt the butter over medium heat. Add the figs, cut side down, and sprinkle with the sugar; sauté for 1 minute. Add the orange juice and zest and, moving the skillet back and forth, cook until the sauce becomes glossy, about 1 minute.

2. Remove the skillet from the stove and add the brandy. While standing back, return the skillet to the stove and carefully tilt it slightly away from the body to ignite the alcohol. (If you do not have a gas stove, carefully ignite the brandy with a match held at the edge of the skillet, tilting it slightly away from the body.) Move the skillet back and forth constantly until the flames die out.

3. To serve, place a scoop of vanilla ice cream in each of 4 bowls. Divide the figs and juices between the bowls and serve immediately.

# Granny Smith Apple Flan

Yield: 8 servings

### Sweet Tart Shell

1 cup/115g cake flour
1 tablespoon sugar
½ cup plus 2 tablespoons/150g unsalted butter, cut into small pieces

1 large egg, beaten
⅛ teaspoon salt
2 tablespoons ice water, or as needed

1. In a large bowl, combine the flour and sugar. Using your fingertips, work the butter into the flour until the mixture resembles coarse meal. Add the egg and salt. Add the water a little at a time (you may not need it all), stirring with a fork until the mixture forms a dough. Pat the dough into a cylinder and chill, covered with plastic wrap, for at least 1 hour or up to 3 days.

2. Preheat the oven to 400°F/200°C. On a lightly floured surface, roll out the dough into an 13-inch/32.5 cm round. Drape the dough over a rolling pin and fit it into a 12-inch/30cm tart pan. Press the dough into the sides of the pan. Prick the shell all over with the tines of a fork to prevent bubbling during baking.

3. Place a piece of aluminum foil over the dough and fill it with pie weights or beans. Place the shell in the oven and bake for 25 minutes, or until lightly golden. Remove from the oven, place on a wire rack, and let cool.

### Pastry Cream

1 cup/250ml whole milk
½ vanilla bean, split
½ cup/120g sugar

2 large egg yolks
2 tablespoons cornstarch

1. In a medium saucepan, bring the milk to a boil. Reduce the heat to low and use the tip of a blunt knife to scrape the vanilla bean seeds into the milk. Gently simmer, stirring occasionally, until the vanilla has infused the milk, about 15 minutes.

2. Meanwhile, in a mixing bowl, whisk the sugar and egg yolks until lightly colored, about 2 minutes. Sift the cornstarch over the mixture and continue whisking until just incorporated. Slowly pour half of the vanilla-infused milk into the egg yolk mixture, gently whisking until well blended.

3. Prepare a large bowl of ice water. Return the egg yolk mixture to the saucepan and place over medium-low heat. Gently cook, stirring continually with a wooden spoon, until the mixture becomes thick and creamy, about 5 minutes. Immediately remove the mixture from the heat and strain through a fine sieve into a medium bowl. Place the bowl in the bowl of ice water to chill the mixture quickly.

4. When the mixture is cool, press a piece of plastic wrap onto the surface to prevent a skin from forming until ready to use.

## To Assemble

1 ½  pounds/680g Granny Smith apples, peeled, cored,
    and sliced very thinly
3  tablespoons/45g unsalted butter, melted

¼  cup/60ml apricot preserves
1  tablespoon water

1. Preheat the oven to 350°F/180°C. Spread a ½-inch/1.25cm-thick layer of pastry cream inside the baked tart shell. Starting from the outside and working in, arrange the apple slices on the pastry cream. Continue, alternating apple layers and pastry cream until you reach the top of the tart shell.

2. With a pastry brush, brush the apple slices lightly with the melted butter. Bake the flan for 20 minutes, or until the apples are golden brown. Transfer the pan to a wire rack and let cool slightly.

3. In a small saucepan, heat the preserves and water over medium heat. With a pastry brush, brush the top of the tart lightly with the melted preserves. Let cool to room temperature, cover, and chill in the refrigerator until ready to serve.

# Peach-Walnut Tart

YIELD: 8 SERVINGS

### Walnut Filling

1 cup/225g sugar
6 tablespoons heavy cream

6 tablespoons whole milk
1 ½ cups/180g chopped walnuts

1. Pour the sugar into a medium heavy saucepan and place it over medium-high heat. Cook, stirring occasionally, until a light caramel forms. While carefully standing back from the saucepan, add the cream and stir until well combined.

2. Add the milk to the mixture and mix thoroughly. Add the walnuts and stir until combined. Cook, stirring, until a candy thermometer registers 225°F/110°C. (If you do not have a candy thermometer, make certain the sugar does not get too dark and burn.) Immediately remove the caramel from the heat and pour it into a clean bowl. Let cool to room temperature. You will have leftover filling; store in the refrigerator covered with plastic wrap.

### Almond Cream

4 ½ tablespoons/70g unsalted butter
5 tablespoons sugar
½ cup/65g almond flour (available at gourmet stores)

1 small egg
2 tablespoons all-purpose flour

In a large mixing bowl, combine the butter, sugar, and almond flour. With an electric mixer on medium speed, beat until light and fluffy, about 5 minutes. (The mixture will appear dry and sandy until the butter begins to incorporate.) Add the egg and beat for 1 minute, stopping 2 or 3 times to scrape down the sides of the bowl. Sift the flour over the batter. With a rubber spatula, fold the flour in gently. Set aside.

### Sugar Dough

6 tablespoons/90g unsalted butter, cut into small pieces
1 large egg
⅓ cup/50g confectioners' sugar

1 ¼ cups/145g cake flour
1 ½ teaspoons baking powder

1. Combine the butter and egg in a mixing bowl. Beat with an electric mixer on medium speed until it resembles scrambled eggs, 2 to 3 minutes. Add the confectioners' sugar and beat for 30 seconds, stopping once to scrape down the sides of the bowl.

2. Add the flour and baking powder and mix just until the dough is smooth and holds together. Turn out onto a lightly floured surface and pat into a disk. Chill, wrapped with plastic wrap, for 1 hour.

3. Roll out the dough into an 12-inch/30cm round about ¼ inch/6mm thick. Drape the dough over a rolling pin and fit it into a 10-inch/25cm tart pan. Press the dough into the sides of the pan. Prick the shell all over with the tines of a fork to prevent bubbling during baking. Cover and chill in the refrigerator until ready to use.

## To Assemble and Bake

*4 to 5 ripe yellow peaches, pitted and thinly sliced*
*1 tablespoon sugar*

*1 tablespoon confectioners' sugar*

1. Preheat the oven to 400°F/200°C. Spread a ¼-inch/6mm-thick layer of almond cream inside the prepared tart shell. Starting from the outside and working in, arrange concentric circles of overlapping peach slices on the almond cream, leaving an open 2-inch/5cm-diameter circle in the center of the tart.

2. Spoon some walnut filling into the center of the tart. Sprinkle the tart with the sugar and bake for 20 to 25 minutes. Transfer the pan to a wire rack and let cool completely.

3. To serve, place the confectioners' sugar in a sieve and sprinkle it over the top of the tart.

---

# Lady Fingers

YIELD: 80 LADY FINGERS

*12 large eggs, separated*
*1 ½ cups/345g sugar*
*1 tablespoon grated lemon zest*

*1 teaspoon pure vanilla extract*
*3 cups/340g cake flour*
*½ cup/70g confectioners' sugar*

1. In a wide saucepan, bring about 1 inch/2.5cm of water to a simmer. Adjust heat so that water is at a bare simmer. In a large heatproof mixing bowl that can sit on the saucepan, combine the egg yolks, ½ cup/120g sugar, lemon zest, and vanilla. Set the bowl over the pan and whisk constantly until the mixture thickens and is lemony looking and an instant-read thermometer registers 110°F/43°C. Remove from the heat and continue to whisk until the bowl no longer feels warm. Set aside.

2. Place the egg whites in a clean, grease-free mixing bowl. With an electric mixer, beat on low speed until frothy. Increase the speed to medium and gradually add the remaining sugar. When the sugar is incorporated, increase the speed to medium-high and beat until the whites hold stiff, glossy peaks.

3. Spoon one-fourth of the egg whites onto the yolk mixture and gently mix in until the batter is lighter. Fold in the remaining egg whites without deflating them until well combined. Sift the cake flour through a sieve over the batter. Fold in gently but thoroughly.

4. Preheat the oven to 400°F/200°C. Line 2 baking sheets with parchment paper. Using a pastry bag fitted with a ½-inch/1.25cm plain tip, pipe out the batter in strips that are ½ inch/1.25cm wide and 3 inches/7.5cm long and spaced 1 inch/2.5cm apart. Place the confectioners' sugar in a medium sieve and sprinkle the strips of batter well and evenly with the sugar. Bake for 5 minutes, or until the lady fingers are firm but still slightly spongy when pressed with a finger. Transfer to a wire rack and let cool on the parchment before removing from the paper. These can be served with Chocolate Mousse (page 122) or dipped in chocolate sauce (page 154).

# champagne

# breakfasts

*Nothing says "I love you" more than breakfast in bed, especially when you're serving a seductive stack of Lovers' Pancakes with Honey and Fruits.*

# Lovers' Pancakes
# with Honey and Fruits

YIELD: 2 SERVINGS

2 cups/225g self-rising cake flour (no substitutions)

¼ cup/60g sugar

1 ⅓ cups/325ml buttermilk

4 tablespoons/60g unsalted butter, melted

2 large eggs

1 teaspoon pure vanilla extract

1 large spoonful whipped cream

1 cherry

½ cup/125ml honey or syrup

1 cup/170g mixed berries (raspberries, blueberries, or strawberries)

1. Mix the flour and sugar together in a bowl. In a separate bowl, combine the buttermilk, butter, eggs, and vanilla. Pour the wet mixture into the dry ingredients and whisk until barely combined. Let sit for 15 minutes.

2. Heat a nonstick skillet over medium heat until hot. Spoon a couple of heaping tablespoons of batter into the center of the skillet, varying the amount of batter depending on the size of the pancake you prefer. If making silver-dollar pancakes, cook 3 at a time. Check the underside of the pancakes with a spatula. When golden brown, flip and continue to cook until browned on both sides.

3. Stack the finished pancakes; top them with a generous dollop of whipped cream and the cherry. Drizzle the stack with the honey and garnish the plate with the berries. Share these pancakes with your lover.

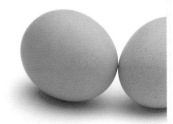

## eggs

Men and women have appreciated the procreative nature of the humble egg for thousands of years. Artists have always been intrigued by its perfect form; chefs have discovered endless methods to prepare it (the French document 685 ways); and lovers still note its invigorating effect. Vatsayana of India outlined many egg-based recipes for love in the *Kama Sutra*, the classical Hindu text that has guided readers in sexual matters since it was written sometime between the third century B.C. and the third century A.D. Indian, Chinese, and Arab manuals all advise the copious consumption of eggs—and not all of them laid by chickens; the *Kama Sutra* recommends sparrow eggs. Today the Japanese favor rich quail eggs, while Filipinos patiently give their eggs a bit more time in the nest, as they believe duck embryos are a source of sexual vitality. That eggs do not merely *symbolize* fertility but are in fact the essence of reproduction itself serves as a reminder that aphrodisiacs were once sought after not just for physical pleasure but to beget children. Thus, a couple perceives something at once earthy and pure when they feed each other simply prepared eggs the morning after an intimate interlude.

# Scrambled Eggs with Caviar

YIELD: 2 SERVINGS

*4 large eggs*
*3 tablespoons heavy cream*
*Salt and freshly ground black pepper to taste*

*2 tablespoons/30g unsalted butter*
*2 ounces/60g sevruga caviar*
*8 slices bread, toasted, buttered, and cut into quarters*

1. In a medium mixing bowl, beat the eggs and cream until just blended. Season with salt and pepper.

2. In a medium nonstick skillet, melt the butter over medium heat. Pour in the beaten egg mixture, increase the heat to medium-high, and stir vigilantly with a wooden spoon until the eggs thicken, about 3 minutes. Remove from the heat.

3. Divide the eggs between 2 warmed plates and top with some caviar. Serve immediately, accompanied with the toast points.

# Caviar Omelet

YIELD: 2 SERVINGS

6  large eggs
    Salt and freshly ground black pepper to taste
2  tablespoons/30g unsalted butter

½  cup/125ml crème fraîche (page 16) or sour cream
2  tablespoons salmon caviar, plus extra for garnish

1. In a small mixing bowl, beat the eggs until just blended. (Do not overbeat.) Season with salt and pepper. Divide into 2 equal portions.

2. Heat a 7-inch/18cm nonstick skillet over medium heat for 3 to 4 minutes. (Do not let the pan get too hot.) Add the butter and swirl to coat the pan. Pour in 1 batch of the beaten eggs. With a wooden spoon, stir the eggs until thickened, about 4 minutes. Let the omelet cook without stirring for 30 seconds. Flip the omelet. (Alternatively, with a spatula, lift up the edges of the omelet and tilt the skillet so that any uncooked egg can run to the bottom of the skillet and cook.) The bottom of the omelet should not be allowed to turn golden.

3. When the omelet is set and soft but not runny, take the pan off the heat and spoon the crème fraîche (or sour cream) and caviar down the center of the omelet. Fold one-third of the omelet over the filling. Tilt the skillet near a warmed plate so that the unfolded edge slides onto the plate; with a rubber spatula, roll the folded edge on top of the unfolded edge, giving the omelet a cigar shape. Repeat from step 2 up to this point with the remaining egg portion. Top the finished omelets with a generous portion of caviar and serve immediately.

# Eggs Benedict with Smoked Salmon

YIELD: 6 SERVINGS

## Hollandaise Sauce

2 large egg yolks
1 stick/120g unsalted butter, melted
Salt and freshly ground black pepper to taste

Cayenne pepper or Tabasco sauce to taste
1 tablespoon fresh lemon juice

1. In the bottom of a double boiler, bring about 1 inch/2.5cm of water to a simmer. Adjust the heat so that the water is at a bare simmer and not boiling. In the top of the double boiler and off the heat, whisk the egg yolks until pale in color and thickened.

2. Position the top of the double boiler over the simmering water and whisk the yolks constantly until thickened. (The bottom of the pan should be visible after whisking, without the eggs running over the whisk's path.)

3. Remove the top of the double boiler from the heat and place it on a folded kitchen towel. While whisking constantly, slowly add the melted butter a tablespoon at a time, whisking well after each addition. Season with salt, pepper, cayenne or Tabasco, and lemon juice. Reserve and keep warm.

## Eggs Benedict

1 tablespoon white wine vinegar
2 large eggs
1 English muffin, split
1 tablespoon/15g unsalted butter, softened

2 slices smoked salmon
2 tablespoons salmon or Russian caviar
2 sprigs dill

1. Fill a 2-quart/2l saucepan almost to the top with water. Bring to a simmer over medium heat and stir in the vinegar. Crack the eggs, one by one, into a cup and carefully pour each egg into the simmering water. Poach the eggs until the desired doneness—about 4 minutes for soft poached, 5 to 6 minutes for medium, and 9 or more minutes for hard. Meanwhile, toast and butter the English muffin.

2. To serve, place an English muffin half on each of 2 warmed plates. Top each half with a slice of salmon. With a slotted spoon, drain the poached eggs, blotting each briefly on paper towels while still in the spoon, and transfer 1 egg to each English muffin half. Spoon 2 tablespoons hollandaise sauce over each egg and top with 1 tablespoon salmon caviar. Garnish with dill sprigs and serve immediately.

# Scrambled Eggs with Tomato and Scallions

YIELD: 2 SERVINGS

1 ripe beefsteak tomato
4 tablespoons/60g unsalted butter
2 scallions, thinly sliced
4 large eggs, lightly beaten

½ cup/40g shredded sharp cheddar, colby,
    or Monterey Jack cheese
Salt and freshly ground black pepper to taste

1. In a small saucepan, bring 2 cups/500ml water to a boil. Meanwhile, with a paring knife, cut out the stem from the tomato and make a small "X" in the opposite end. Plunge the tomato in the boiling water and leave it in just until the skin is loosened, 10 to 20 seconds. With a slotted spoon, remove the tomato and rinse it under cold water until cool enough to handle. Slip off the skin and cut the tomato in half. Gently but firmly squeeze the seeds from the tomato halves. Cut into small dice.

2. In a small skillet, heat 2 tablespoons/30g butter over high heat. Add the tomato and scallions and cook, stirring, for 2 minutes. Transfer the vegetables to a small bowl and set aside.

3. In the same skillet, heat the remaining 2 tablespoons/30g butter over high heat. Pour in the beaten eggs, reduce the heat to low, and stir vigilantly until the eggs turn creamy. Gently fold in the reserved tomato and scallions. Immediately remove from the heat.

4. To serve, spoon a heap of the scrambled eggs on each of 2 warmed plates. Sprinkle with the cheese, season with salt and pepper, and serve immediately.

# Champagne Cocktail

2 teaspoons superfine sugar

4 drops Angostura bitters

12 ounces (1 ½ cups)/375ml champagne, Deutz champagne preferred

2 splashes brandy

2 slices orange

Combine 1 teaspoon sugar and 2 drops bitters in each of 2 champagne glasses. Swirl to combine. Add 6 ounces/185ml of champagne and a splash of brandy to each glass. Garnish the glasses with the orange slices.

# Hot Chocolate with Whipped Cream

YIELD: 2 SERVINGS

½ cup/125ml heavy cream

2 cups/500ml whole milk

½ cup/40g unsweetened cocoa powder

2 ounces (¼ cup)/60ml rum (optional)

Shaved chocolate for garnish

1. In a chilled large mixing bowl, whip the cream until soft peaks form. Set aside.

2. In a small saucepan, bring the milk to a boil over medium heat. Add the cocoa and cook, stirring, until thickened. Remove from the heat and divide between 2 mugs. Add a shot of rum to each if desired. Garnish each mug with a dollop of the whipped cream and some chocolate shavings.

## champagne

No prelude to romance builds anticipation quite like the whispered whoosh of a champagne cork gently removed. True champagne, the sparkling wine made only in the Champagne region of northern France, contains chardonnay, pinot noir, and (usually) pinot meunier grapes, which somehow thrive in the chilly climate and chalky soil. Throughout history well-known romantic figures such as Casanova (1725–98) and the dancer Isadora Duncan (1877–1927) favored champagne, and literature and film also celebrate champagne as the sensual libation. Remember Leslie Caron and Louis Jourdan in *Gigi*?

You already know that brut (dry) champagne is the perfect accompaniment to oysters, caviar, salmon, and foie gras. But have you tried it with egg dishes, fried foods, and spicy Asian cuisine? Surprise your partner! Remember to pair desserts with *demi-sec* or *doux* bottlings, as sweet treats make dry wines taste sour. For best results, pour well-chilled champagne (45°F/7°C) into two flutes, look into your lover's eyes, and recall "the night they invented champagne."

# cocktails

*Enjoy your aphrodisiac feast with one of these cocktails and make a toast to an evening filled with sensory pleasures.*

# Bloody Mary

YIELD: 2 COCKTAILS

10  regular-size ice cubes
 3  ounces (6 tablespoons)/75ml vodka
 1  cup/250ml tomato juice
    Juice of 1 lemon
 4  dashes Worcestershire sauce
 2  dashes Tabasco sauce

 2  pinches bottled horseradish
    Freshly ground black pepper to taste
 2  stalks celery, with leaves
 2  wedges lemon
 2  pickled green beans

In a shaker, combine the ice cubes and vodka. Cover and shake vigorously. Add the tomato juice, lemon juice, Worcestershire sauce, Tabasco sauce, and horseradish. Shake again and strain into 2 wine glasses. Sprinkle each with the pepper and garnish with celery, lemon wedge, and pickled green bean.

---

# Pussy Foot

YIELD: 2 COCKTAILS

12 to 14  regular-size ice cubes
    ½  cup/125ml fresh orange juice
    ½  cup/125ml fresh lemon juice
    ½  cup/125ml fresh lime juice
    2  dashes grenadine

    1  large egg yolk, beaten lightly (optional)
    2  splashes soda water
    2  maraschino cherries
    2  slices orange

In a shaker, combine the ice cubes, orange juice, lemon juice, lime juice, grenadine, and egg yolk if using. Cover and shake vigorously. Strain into 2 medium glasses. Add a splash of soda water to each glass and garnish with a maraschino cherry and an orange slice.

## horseradish

The sharp bite of this root brings a quivering to the nose and a tear to the eye. In Greek mythology the Delphic oracle told Apollo that horseradish was worth its weight in gold, establishing its relative value for centuries. And although Jews pronounce horseradish as one of the five "bitter herbs" at the springtime Passover seder, it inspires affection between men and women—a scenario not at all bitter and quite holy indeed.

# Screwdriver

YIELD: 2 COCKTAILS

4 ounces (1/2 cup)/125ml vodka

1 cup/250ml fresh orange juice

10 regular-size ice cubes

2 slices orange

In a shaker, combine the vodka and orange juice. Cover and shake vigorously. Divide the ice cubes between 2 tall glasses. Pour the orange juice and vodka over the ice. Garnish with the orange slices.

# White Russian

YIELD: 2 COCKTAILS

16 regular-size ice cubes

3 ounces (6 tablespoons)/75ml vodka

3 ounces (6 tablespoons)/75ml Kahlúa

6 tablespoons heavy cream

Divide the ice cubes between 2 old fashioned glasses. Divide and add the remaining ingredients to the glasses. Stir slightly and serve.

# Ginseng Cocktail

YIELD: 2 COCKTAILS

2 fresh ginseng roots, soaked in 1 liter whiskey or brandy for at least 1 week

2 ounces/60ml dry vermouth

½ teaspoon sugar syrup

2 orange slices

2 maraschino cherries

Use 2 ounces/60ml of whiskey per cocktail. Divide and add the vermouth and syrup to the drinks. Stir slightly, garnish with the orange slices and cherries, and serve.

## ginseng

The Koreans and Chinese saw in the forked shape of *Panax ginseng* the form of a human body, meaning that this root would regulate the entire system. Hence, ginseng is celebrated for its positive effect on memory, digestion, pulmonary health, and longevity. Asians reserve their highest regard, however, for the root's effect on sexual vitality; why else would enthusiasts eat it and drink liquids made from it each day? Chinese Taoists found that ginseng enhanced the harmonious balance of male (yang) and female (yin) elements during lovemaking, bringing both partners closer to the spirit of the universe. A cup of ginseng tea together by the light of the moon may inspire your yin and yang to intermingle as well.

# midnight

*After a romantic evening, share Smoked Salmon on Dark Bread or a Shrimp Cocktail with your lover.*

# snacks

*These midnight snacks will let you feast in style.*

# oysters

When beautiful Aphrodite sprang forth from the sea on an oyster shell, she lent these bivalve mollusks her penchant for rapture, making them the most glorious, exalted, love food of all. The Romans feasted on oysters during their orgies and wrote of their hedonistic merits, validated by lovers for centuries. Many have idolized the asymmetrical shell for its stunning resemblance to the woman's sexual organs, especially when a well-placed pearl rests suggestively between the two halves.

What's more, recent research underscores ancient wisdom, as oysters contain high quantities of zinc, several times more than any other edible substance. The connection between zinc and sex is that most of a man's zinc is stored in the testes, where it is needed for the synthesis of dihydroxytestosterone (DHT), an active enzyme of testosterone. Concentrations of zinc are also found in the pineal and hippocampus glands of men and women, which influence libido and emotions. Studies have also revealed that oysters contain dopamine, a neurotransmitter that influences sexual desire and intensifies sensation. If nothing else, the succulence of the oyster is sure to be a turn-on. Served raw on the half shell, a fresh oyster should be plump, creamy in color, and sweet smelling, swimming in its own clear liquor. Keep a cagey eye out for the famed belon oysters if you ever take that second honeymoon in Europe!

# Oysters with Caviar

YIELD: 2 SERVINGS

12 *fresh oysters*
6 *ounces/180g caviar*

*Crushed ice*
*Lemon wedges (optional)*

Wash and drain the oysters in a colander in the sink. Open each shell with an oyster knife or can opener.

Top each oyster with some caviar. Serve immediately on crushed ice with lemon wedges if desired.

# Classic Caviar

YIELD: 2 SERVINGS

1 *large egg, hard boiled*
2 *tablespoons sour cream*
1 *lemon, quartered*
½ *small onion, finely chopped*

4 *tablespoons/60g beluga caviar, chilled*
2 *slices two-day-old good-quality bread, toasted, crusts trimmed, buttered, and cut into quarters*

1. Chop the egg white and egg yolk separately; place each in a small bowl. Place the sour cream, lemon wedges, and onion in separate bowls.

2. Spoon some caviar in the center of 2 chilled plates. Surround with the bowls of egg white, egg yolk, sour cream, onion, and lemon. Serve, accompanied by the toast points.

# Shrimp Cocktail

YIELD: 2 SERVINGS

¼ cup/5g shredded mesclun

8 large shrimp, cooked, peeled, deveined, and chilled

2 cherry tomatoes, cut into wedges

2 lemon wedges

4 whole salad leaves for garnish, such as red leaf lettuce

2 sprigs dill

Hot Cocktail Sauce (recipe below)

Place the shredded salad leaves on the bottom of 2 martini glasses. Place 4 shrimp on the rim of each glass and garnish decoratively with lemon wedges, salad leaves, and dill sprigs. Serve with hot cocktail sauce.

## Hot Cocktail Sauce

YIELD: ABOUT 1 CUP

¼ cup/60ml chili sauce

½ cup/125ml ketchup

3 tablespoons grated fresh horseradish

2 tablespoons Worcestershire sauce

½ teaspoon fresh lemon juice

Tabasco sauce, salt, and pepper to taste

Place all the ingredients in a small bowl and mix thoroughly.

# Smoked Salmon Pizza with Caviar

## caviar

Skeptics who suspect caviar qualifies as an aphrodisiac only because of its rarity, beware! Defenders of sturgeon roe adamantly swear by its erotic potency, matched only by the delight in popping it between the tongue and palate to release its delicate, briny flavor. The sturgeon is an animal of prehistoric physical nature and proportions. A fish may live more than a century and weigh over a ton; it has plates, not scales. Beluga, the biggest sturgeon, produces the largest, most highly prized eggs. Both osetra and sevruga have smaller eggs ranging from black to brown to gold; the golden eggs were once reserved for the courts of the Russian czar and the Iranian shah. All caviar is salted to preserve the temperamental eggs; look on the jar or tin for the Russian word *malossol*, meaning "lightly salted," indicating a very high grade. You and your paramour will benefit from caviar's high phosphorus and iron content, as well as from the ritual of serving it chilled on ice, taking tender care to not damage a single egg. Rigorous guides ban the use of metal spoons or other silverware. Either splurge on mother-of-pearl or get creative, scooping up the last tidbits with your lover's finger.

### Dough

1 ⅔  cups/200g all-purpose flour
¼  cup/30g whole-wheat flour
1  tablespoon semolina flour
¾  cup/200ml warm water (90° to 100°F/32° to 38°C)

2  teaspoons olive oil
1  teaspoon active dry yeast
1  teaspoon honey
½  teaspoon salt

1. In a medium bowl, combine the all-purpose, whole-wheat, and semolina flours. In a glass measuring cup, mix the remaining ingredients. Make a well in the dry ingredients and pour in the wet ingredients. With a wooden spoon, mix the wet ingredients from the center outward until the dough becomes smooth and elastic.

2. Turn the dough out onto a lightly floured surface and knead for 6 minutes. Place the dough in a well-oiled bowl, turning to coat it on all sides, and cover with plastic wrap. Place in a warm place (75°F/24°C) for 4 to 6 hours. The pizza dough can be made in advance up to this point, especially if it's for a midnight snack.

### Topping

4  tablespoons olive oil
½  medium red onion, cut into rings
½  cup/125ml crème fraîche (page 16) or sour cream
6  ounces/180g smoked salmon, thinly sliced (about 6 slices)

4  sprigs dill, chopped
   Freshly ground black pepper to taste
2  tablespoons salmon roe
2  teaspoons black caviar

1. Preheat the oven to 350°F/180°C. On a lightly floured surface, roll out the dough into a 6-inch/15cm round. Prick the dough all over with the tines of a fork and brush with 1 tablespoon olive oil. Bake on a pizza stone or baking sheet for 12 to 14 minutes, or until lightly browned on the edges and slightly crispy. Remove from the oven and let cool slightly. Keep warm.

2. Meanwhile, in a medium skillet, heat 1 tablespoon olive oil over medium heat. Add the onion and reduce the heat to low; cook slowly, stirring occasionally, until golden and caramelized. Remove from the heat.

3. To serve, spread the crème fraîche or sour cream evenly over the warm pizza crust. Arrange the smoked salmon over the crème fraîche. Top with the caramelized onion and sprinkle with the dill and the pepper. Randomly spoon the salmon roe and the black caviar over the pizza. Lightly drizzle with the remaining 2 tablespoons olive oil and serve immediately.

# Smoked Salmon on Dark Bread

YIELD: 2 SERVINGS

½ pound/225g thinly sliced top-quality Norwegian
  smoked salmon

4 thin slices dark bread, crusts removed

½ small lemon, quartered

2 sprigs dill

Fan the slices of salmon down the left side on each of 2 plates. Place 2 slices bread on the right side of each plate. Garnish with a lemon wedge and dill sprig and serve immediately.

# Tricolore Salsas

YIELD: 4 SERVINGS PER SALSA

### Tomatillo Salsa

8 tomatillos, husked, cored, and cut into ¼-inch dice

2 scallions, chopped

2 serrano chiles, seeded and finely chopped

2 cloves garlic, roasted

1 tablespoon chopped fresh cilantro

1 teaspoon fresh lime juice

Salt to taste

In a medium nonreactive bowl, combine all the ingredients except the salt. Toss to combine well.

Season with salt. Let sit for 30 minutes before serving.

### Red Tomato Salsa

4 small ripe tomatoes, cored, seeded, and cut
  into ¼-inch/6mm dice

½ small red onion, cut into ¼-inch/6mm dice

2 tablespoons diced red bell pepper

1 red jalapeño pepper, seeded and finely chopped

2 cloves garlic, roasted

1 teaspoon fresh lime juice

Salt to taste

In a medium nonreactive bowl, combine all the ingredients except the salt. Toss to combine well.

Season with salt. Let sit for 30 minutes before serving.

### Yellow Tomato Salsa

4 small yellow tomatoes, cored, seeded, and cut into
  ¼-inch/6mm dice, or 1 pint/225g yellow
  cherry tomatoes, diced

2 serrano chiles, seeded and finely chopped

3 tablespoons diced mango

2 tablespoons diced yellow bell pepper

2 tablespoons fresh orange juice

Salt to taste

In a medium nonreactive bowl, combine all the ingredients except the salt. Toss to combine well.

Season with salt. Let sit for 30 minutes before serving.

## tomatoes

Perhaps no other aphrodisiac defines the romance of summer quite like luscious ripe tomatoes. Next time you are browsing the produce section in January or February, compare the scent of a Holland stem tomato (yes, one of those pricey, bright red babies) to that of a "hothouse" tomato (ripened in a Mack truck somewhere between California and your hometown). Smell the difference? Does the one with the gently curving stem remind you of frolicking with your mate on a picnic blanket? Of sunnier days spent gardening side by side, your bare arms casually brushing as you make your way between the vines?

Tomatoes acquired their sexy standing in a roundabout fashion. The Spanish brought them to Europe from the New World in the sixteenth century, where they received a cold reception—even in Spain. The French mistranslated the plant's Latin name, meaning "apple of the Moors" as *pomme de mort*. The English, in turn, misunderstood this as *pomme d'amour*, or "apple of love." Thus the English believed tomatoes to be doubly dangerous, not only poisonous but also morally corrupting. Caress the smooth, red skin before slicing and serving as an appetizer with olive oil and black pepper. Play footsie under the table. It's summer again.

# Shrimp Cocktail

YIELD: 2 SERVINGS

¼ cup/5g shredded mesclun

8 large shrimp, cooked, peeled, deveined, and chilled

2 cherry tomatoes, cut into wedges

2 lemon wedges

4 whole salad leaves for garnish, such as red leaf lettuce

2 sprigs dill

Hot Cocktail Sauce (recipe below)

Place the shredded salad leaves on the bottom of 2 martini glasses. Place 4 shrimp on the rim of each glass and garnish decoratively with lemon wedges, salad leaves, and dill sprigs. Serve with hot cocktail sauce.

## Hot Cocktail Sauce

YIELD: ABOUT 1 CUP

¼ cup/60ml chili sauce

½ cup/125ml ketchup

3 tablespoons grated fresh horseradish

2 tablespoons Worcestershire sauce

½ teaspoon fresh lemon juice

Tabasco sauce, salt, and pepper to taste

Place all the ingredients in a small bowl and mix thoroughly.

# Steak Tartare with Caviar and Quail Eggs

YIELD: 2 SERVINGS

*1 pound/454g beef tenderloin, trimmed of all*
  *fat and sinew*
*3 tablespoons finely chopped red onion*
*2 tablespoons finely chopped sour gherkins*
*1 tablespoon finely chopped fresh parsley*
*6 anchovy fillets, finely chopped*
*1 tablespoon capers, rinsed, drained, and chopped*
*1 large egg yolk*

*Tabasco sauce to taste*
*Worcestershire sauce to taste*
*Pinch paprika*
*Dash brandy*
*Salt and freshly ground black pepper to taste*
*2 tablespoons black or Russian caviar*
*1 quail egg, hard boiled, peeled, and split in half*
*1 sprig parsley*

1. With a sharp knife, finely chop the tenderloin and place it in a large bowl. Add the onion, gherkins, chopped parsley, anchovy, capers, and egg yolk; stir until well combined. Season with the Tabasco, Worcestershire, paprika, brandy, salt, and pepper. Cover and chill in the refrigerator for at least 30 minutes until ready to use.

2. Mold the chilled steak mixture into one large 6-inch/15cm patty. Top with half a quail egg, and top the egg with the caviar. Use the other egg half to garnish the plate along with the parsley sprig. Feed the steak tartare to your significant other.

# chocolate

Ah, chocolate, the last word in decadence. Montezuma, the Aztec emperor, drank 50 goblets of hot chocolate a day for the stamina he needed to satisfy his many wives. The Aztecs flavored their *chocolatl* with chile peppers, another New World aphrodisiac. The sensuous stimulant also caught on among Europe's royal courts, known for their tendency toward lascivious intrigue. Today the average American consumes 10 to 12 pounds of chocolate annually. You need no convincing; you felt chocolate's libidinous effect when you exchanged foil-wrapped kisses on Valentine's Day or when you shared a batch of piping hot, gooey brownies. And now scientists agree. Chocolate combines both theobromine, a mild relative of caffeine, and magnesium, a calmative. Recently they also found traces of phenylethylamine (PEA), a substance released by the brain when in love. Adding to the enchantment, chocolate candy melts at a temperature near your own, so those solid morsels are transformed into a divine liquid in the mouth. So when the two of you indulge together, be prepared for a meltdown.

# Chocolate Truffles

YIELD: 25 TRUFFLES

20 ounces/570g bittersweet (not unsweetened) chocolate, chopped
⅔ cup/150ml heavy cream

4 tablespoons/60g unsalted butter
8 ounces/225g unsweetened cocoa powder, preferably Dutch-process

1. Place half of the chocolate in a mixing bowl. In a small saucepan, bring the cream to a boil over medium heat. Pour the cream over the chocolate and whisk until the chocolate is smooth and no small lumps remain. Stir in the butter and whisk until melted. Pour the mixture onto a stainless-steel baking sheet and let stand for at least 4 hours.

2. Scoop the mixture up by tablespoonfuls and roll into balls. Place the truffles on a baking sheet.

3. Place the remaining chocolate in the top of a double boiler set over 1 inch/2.5cm of simmering (not boiling) water. Whisk until the chocolate is smooth and no small lumps remain.

4. Place the cocoa powder in a sieve and sprinkle it over a tray. Spoon some of the melted chocolate into your hand and roll a truffle in it until completely covered. Roll the truffle in the cocoa and place on a serving tray. Repeat with the remaining truffles. Place the truffles in a cool place and enjoy at midnight with a glass of champagne.

# Index

Page numbers for illustrations are in *italics*.

194